THE PURE TIME-PREFERENCE
THEORY OF INTEREST

The Pure Time-Preference Theory of Interest

{ *Edited by Jeffrey M. Herbener* }

MISES INSTITUTE

Copyright © 2011 by the Ludwig von Mises Institute
Published under Creative Commons Attribution 3.0.
http://creativecommons.org/licenses/by/3.0/

Ludwig von Mises Institute
518 West Magnolia Avenue
Auburn, Alabama 36832
Mises.org

ISBN: 978-1-61016-236-4

Contents

7	Foreword by Douglas E. French
11	Introduction by Jeffrey M. Herbener
59	Time Preference *By Murray N. Rothbard*
67	Human Action: The Rate of Interest *By Ludwig von Mises*
85	In Defense of the Misesian Theory of Interest *By Roger W. Garrison*
99	The Pure Time-Preference Theory of Interest: An Attempt at Clarification *By Israel M. Kirzner*
127	Interest Theories, Old and New *By Frank A. Fetter*
159	Professor Rothbard and the Theory of Interest *By Roger W. Garrison*
173	Bibliography
181	Index

Foreword

Consumers and entrepreneurs often speak of "the cost of money" when referring to interest rates. Modern lenders also refer to the interest they charge as "loan pricing." Viewed this way, interest is viewed as if it were any other good. The cheaper a good the more affordable it is. And so the lower the interest rate, the more affordable. By dictating key interest rates, modern central bankers are believed to be alchemists, lowering interest rates to magically transform scarcity into prosperity.

As the world struggles to deleverage, with the market constantly forced to clear malinvestments of a continuous string of asset bubbles and crashes, central bankers continue their faith in the ancient tradition. All the economy needs is more monetary elixir. If the patient hasn't yet responded, it must mean larger doses are needed: Interest rates must be too high.

The mainstream view has devolved to the belief that zero is too high. In the spring of 2009, Harvard economist, and former adviser to President George W. Bush, N. Gregory Mankiw seriously wrote in the *New York Times*, "It May Be Time for the Fed to Go Negative." But who would lend money to only receive less in return?

Mankiw approvingly cites German economist Silvio Gesell's argument for a tax on holding money, an idea John Maynard Keynes himself approved of. Crazier still is Mankiw's idea that one of his graduate students floated, of turning interest-rate policy into an absurd game of chance.

> Imagine that the Fed were to announce that, a year from today, it would pick a digit from zero to 9 out of a hat. All currency with a serial number ending in that digit would no longer be legal tender. Suddenly, the expected return to holding currency would become negative 10 percent.
>
> That move would free the Fed to cut interest rates below zero. People would be delighted to lend money at negative 3 percent, since losing 3 percent is better than losing 10.
>
> Of course, some people might decide that at those rates, they would rather spend the money—for example, by buying a new car. But because expanding aggregate demand is precisely the goal of the interest rate cut, such an incentive isn't a flaw—it's a benefit.[1]

Mankiw recognizes that the idea of negative interest rates is nonsense to most people. But he writes, "Early mathematicians thought that the idea of negative numbers was absurd. Today, these numbers are commonplace."

However there is nothing new about the idea of the state juicing up an economy with low interest rates. John Law's monetary theory for an ailing France in the early 1700s was built on a foundation of low interest rates. The Scottish economist and policy maker believed interest rates were derived from,

> (1) the quantity of money, (2) the quality of the government, and (3) the security of the state's debt. If the quantity of money increased relative to the demand for it, the government of the country was good, and the state debt secure, then, interest rates would fall.[2]

---

[1] N. Gregory Mankiw, "It May Be Time for the Fed to Go Negative," *New York Times*, April 18, 2009.

[2] Antoin E. Murphy, *John Law: Economic Theorist and Policymaker* (Oxford: Oxford University Press, 1997), p. 65.

The result of Law's monetary experiment was the famous Mississippi Bubble that devastated the French economy. The continuous injections of new money that Law flooded into the market not only rushed into Mississippi Company shares, but into commodities as well, while money wages for the French working class never caught up.

And so it goes today.

However, Keynesians are undeterred in their belief that low interest rates put people back to work and solve all economic woes, albeit with nagging liquidity trap apprehension. Keynes believed the rate of interest is "the reward for parting with liquidity for a specific period … is a measure of the unwillingness of those who possess money to part with their liquid control over it."[3]

Keynes believed that those who hold cash for the speculative motive to be wicked. And it is up to central bankers to stop this evil. However, Henry Hazlitt explained in *The Failure of the "New Economics,"* holding cash balances,

> is usually most indulged in after a boom has cracked. The best way to prevent it is not to have a Monetary Authority so manipulate things as to force the purchase of investments or of goods, but to prevent an inflationary boom in the first place.[4]

Keynes thought money to be barren as a store of wealth while investments yielded returns, writing "Why should anyone outside a lunatic asylum wish to use money as a store of wealth?"

If liquidity preference determined the rate of interest, rates would be lowest during a recovery and at the peak of booms, with confidence high, everyone would be seeking to trade their liquidity for investments in things. "But it is precisely in a recovery and at the peak of a boom that short-term interest rates are highest," Hazlitt writes.

---

3 John Maynard Keynes, *The General Theory of Employment, Interest and Money* (New York: Harcourt, Brace and Company, 1936), p. 167.
4 Henry Hazlitt, *The Failure of the "New Economics"* (Princeton, N.J.: D. Van Nostrand, 1959), p. 190.

Time is what Keynesians leave out of their calculus. While lenders may think they are lending money, they are really lending time. Present goods are more valuable than future goods. Borrowers buy the use of time. Hazlitt reminds us that the old word for interest was usury, "etymologically more descriptive than its modern substitute."

Borrowers pay interest in order to buy present assets. It is time preference that determines interest: the discount of future goods as against present goods. Most importantly, this ratio is outside the reach of the monetary authorities. It is determined subjectively by the actions of millions of market participants.

Central bank manipulation of interest rates can never fix an ailing economy. It is impossible for the monetary authorities to dictate the proper interest rate. Interest rates determined by command and control bear no relation to the collective time preference of economic actors. The result of central bank intervention can only be distortions and chaos.

Those pushing the monetary buttons are naïve in believing they can steer the economy by setting interest policy when, in fact, they don't understand what interest is or how the rate of interest is determined.

The following essays parse through the uniquely Austrian insight of the pure time-preference theory of interest, but more importantly go to the core of why modern central bank monetary engineering leaves the economy further from recovery while at the same time providing a Petri dish for speculation and malinvestment.

Douglas E. French
Auburn, Alabama
July 2011

Introduction

Carl Menger's Approach to Economics

The genius of Carl Menger is seen as much in his perception of where economics needed to go and how it could get there as in his correction of the faulty course set for it by the British Classical economists. In the preface to his *Principles of Economics*, he wrote:

> I have devoted special attention to the investigation of the causal connections between economic phenomena involving products and the corresponding agents of production, not only for the purpose of establishing a price theory based upon reality and placing all price phenomena (including interest, wages, ground rent, etc.) together under one unified point of view, but also because of the important insights we thereby gain into many other economic processes heretofore completely misunderstood.[1]

The caliber of intellectuals in the second and third generations of Menger's followers in the causal-realist tradition, who

---

[1] Carl Menger, *Principles of Economics* (New York: New York University Press, 1976 [1871]), p. 49.

rose to the challenge of building a general theory of economics, testifies to the power of Menger's vision.

Frank Fetter was the first economist to integrate interest theory into a causal-realist conception of economics.[2] In 1914 he wrote, "In an elementary textbook published in 1904 this [i.e., the Pure Time Preference] conception of the interest theory was embodied, not as a thing apart from, but as an integral part of, a general theory of value."[3] Thus, eight years before Ludwig von Mises would integrate money into causal-realist economic theory, Fetter had already integrated interest into Menger's system. Reflecting on what he had accomplished, he wrote:

> This interest theory was new in its *order of development* from elementary choice; in the *priority it assigned to capitalization* above contract interest; in its *unified psychological explanation* of all the phenomena of the surplus that emerges when undervalued expected incomes approach maturity, the surplus all being derived from the value of enjoyable (direct) goods, not by two separate theories, for consumption and production goods respectively; in the *integration* of the interest theory *with the whole theory of distribution*; and in a number of details necessarily related to these features.[4]

The contrast between Menger and William Stanley Jevons on the nature of a general theory of economics could hardly be more vivid. In the preface to the second edition of his *The Theory of Political Economy*, Jevons wrote:

> In fact, the whole subject [i.e., economics] is so extensive, intricate, and diverse, that it is absurd to suppose it can be treated

---

2 Fetter straddled the second and third generations of Austrian economists being born 12 years after Eugen von Böhm-Bawerk and 18 years before Ludwig von Mises.

3 Frank Fetter, "Interest Theories, Old and New," reprinted in this volume, p. 135. Fetter is referring to the first edition of his book, *Principles of Economics* (New York: The Century Co., 1904).

4 Ibid., p. 139. Italics in original.

in any single book or in any single manner. It is no more one science than statics, dynamics, the theory of heat, optics, magnetoelectricity, telegraphy, navigation, and photographic chemistry are one science.[5]

Although Jevons thought that the topics that made up economics could not be integrated into a single theoretical body, he claimed that genuine economic analysis employed a mathematical approach uniformly across all topics. Having initially considered himself a pioneer in this respect, he began to search the history of economic thought for precursors after he published the first edition of *The Theory of Political Economy*. His search convinced him that mathematics has been the method of economists from before the time of Adam Smith onward even if they were unaware of it. So struck was he by his interpretation that he wrote in the preface to the second edition of his book, "Turning now to the theory itself, the question is not so much whether the theory given in this volume is true, but whether there is really any novelty in it."[6]

The thrust of Menger's approach, in contrast, is to discover the causal laws of human action and integrate them into a single coherent system, a body of true propositions that explain the underlying, universal causes of all human action as well as those for each relevant sub-category of human action, consuming, producing, buying, selling, and so on. The wellspring of all economic theory is the reality of the human condition. As a finite being, man makes a distinction between ends and means. He cannot attain his ends by an act of will alone, but must apply means to attain his ends. Man lives in an orderly, but finite world. Using means produces only limited effects in attaining ends. Endowed with reason, man is able to perceive the causal connection between the use of means and the attainment of ends. Any action toward the attainment of an end

---

5 William Stanley Jevons, *The Theory of Political Economy*, 3rd ed. (London: Macmillan, 1888 [1871]), p. xvi.
6 Ibid., p. vii.

requires surrendering the attainment of another end with the same means. And any action using a set of means requires foregoing using another set of means to attain the same end. Action, therefore, requires choice. As a purposeful being, man selects what he perceives to be higher-valued ends to pursue and what he perceives to be lower-valued sets of means to employ. Choice, therefore, requires a judgment of the mind. Since attaining the end is the purpose of an action, the value a person attaches to the attainment of the end is primary. A person attaches only derivative value to the means used in action since they are merely aids to the attainment of the end. Means have no value independent of the value a person attaches to the end they help attain. The human mind imputes value to the means according to the aid they render in attaining a valuable end. The technical properties of each of the means that combine to attain an end can be valued differently by different persons or by the same person at different times and, therefore, have no causal impact on choice and action independent of the judgment of the mind.

As a temporal being, man distinguishes between sooner and later. He can, therefore, judge the value of attaining an end sooner differently than attaining it later. Just as the principle of preference is implied by man's finitude, time preference is implied by his temporality. Temporal beings prefer the satisfaction of an end sooner to the same satisfaction later. Man places a premium on present satisfaction over future satisfaction. Since time preference refers only to the difference in value of the satisfaction of an end sooner instead of the same satisfaction later, the discount a person places on the future will be uniform across all actions with the same intertemporal structure. Moreover, the discount applies to all actions regardless of when a person chooses to undertake any one of them. In choosing to take an action later, a person is demonstrating that the value of the action in the future exceeds its value in the present, even when the discount of the future is applied. His temporal choice, then, conforms to the general principle of action, that he chooses a more-highly valued alternative and foregoes a less-highly valued one. He economizes his actions across all aspects of action subject to choice: ends, means, place, and time.

In short, the human mind integrates all the factors affecting human action into a systematic whole, reconciling the objective, technical features of the world, including time, through judgments of value in a way that renders the highest satisfaction of ends.

The market economy performs this integration for society. Prices are determined by the underlying preferences of buyers and sellers. Objective factors have no independent effect on prices, but influence prices only through preferences. Prices of consumer goods are directly determined by the preferences consumers have for them as expressed in their demands for the goods. Prices of producer goods used to produce each consumer good are indirectly determined by consumer preferences as they generate revenue for entrepreneurs to justify the demand entrepreneurs express for them. Entrepreneurs pay each factor of production the monetary value of its contribution to production. If the factor payment is made sooner than the revenue is received from the sale of the output produced, then the payment is discounted because of time preference. This discount of future money relative to present money is interest and determines the pure, or time preference, rate of interest. Because all exchange of present money for future money of the same time structure involves time preference, the pure rate of interest is uniform across all such intertemporal exchange. It follows that all present goods that generate future money will have their prices determined by discounting the future money by the rate of interest to obtain the equivalent amount of present money. This process of capitalization results in a uniform rate of interest as the difference between the present money spent to acquire factors of production and the future money obtained from selling the output produced. Prices, so determined, are the basis for economic calculation which permits entrepreneurs to appraise the lines of production and investment that people find most valuable.

The followers of Jevons take an entirely different approach.[7] In applying mathematics to the explanation of human action, they formulate mathematical functions among the factors relevant to explain each aspect of human action. Utility functions and budget constraints explain consumer choices of goods. Revenue functions and costs functions determine producer choices of levels of production of output. Demand and supply functions determine prices of goods. Aggregate demand and aggregate supply functions determine aggregate output and employment, and so on. In each analysis, each function has a distinct effect that is combined with the effects described by the other functions to produce the overall effect. There is no integration in the Mengerian sense and certainly the human mind does not integrate every causal factor through judgments of value. Instead, price is jointly determined by consumer utility and production relationships, for example. Interest, being a price, is likewise determined jointly by intertemporal preferences and production relationships.

The Prehistory of the PTPT

Carl Menger formulated the two crucial aspects of the Pure Time-Preference Theory (PTPT) of interest: a present satisfaction is valued above the same satisfaction in the future and capitalization. He developed the first point in his argument that economic progress occurs when productive effort is redirected from goods of lower order to goods of higher order and thereby, longer, more productive production processes. The restraint on economic progress comes from a phenomenon "deeply imbedded in human nature," which is the desire to have present desires satisfied over future desires. This stems not only from pressing physiological needs, but also those things that contribute "merely

---

7 F.A. Hayek makes a similar point in comparing Mises's achievement in integrating money into the marginal utility theory of Menger and Fisher's mathematical version of the quantity theory of money. See Hayek, *Prices and Production and Other Works* (Auburn, Ala.: Ludwig von Mises Institute, 2008), pp. 197–205.

[to] our continued well-being," and even "with satisfactions having merely the importance of enjoyments." Menger wrote, "All experience teaches that a present enjoyment or one in the near future usually appears more important to men than one of equal intensity at a more remote time in the future."[8]

On discounting, Menger wrote:

> Now if, in ordinary life, we see that buyers of goods of higher order never pay the full prospective price of a good of lower order for the complementary means of production technically necessary for its production, that they are always only in a position to grant, and actually do grant, prices for them that are somewhat lower than the price of the product, and that the sale of goods of higher order thus has a certain similarity to discounting, the prospective price of the product forming the basis of the computation, these facts are explained by the preceding argument.[9]

Menger also understood that the time discount operates universally across the production structure and the credit markets. He wrote:

> If he wishes to exchange his goods of higher order immediately for the corresponding goods of lower order, or for what is the same thing under developed trade relations, a corresponding sum of money, he is evidently in a position similar to that of a person who is to receive a certain sum of money at a future point in time (after 6 months, for example) but who wants to obtain command of it immediately. If the owner of goods of higher order intends to transfer them to a third person and is willing to receive payment only after the end of the production process, naturally no "discounting" takes place.[10]

The capital value of an asset, for Menger, is the sum of the value of output it generates discounted to its present value. He wrote:

---

8 Menger, *Principles of Economics*, pp. 153–54.
9 Ibid., pp. 158–59.
10 Ibid., p. 159.

> The aggregate present value of all the complementary quantities of goods of higher order ... necessary for the production of a good of lower or first order is equal to the prospective value of the product.... Hence the *present* value of the technical factors of production by themselves is not equal to the full prospective value of the product, but always behaves in such a way that a margin for the value of the services of capital and entrepreneurial activity remains.[11]

Menger had precursors on these two aspects of the PTPT, as Murray Rothbard discusses in his contribution to this volume. Chief among them was A.R.J. Turgot who understood both time preference and capitalization and their impact on interest. On the premium of present money over future money, Turgot wrote:

> Is not this difference well known, and is not the commonplace proverb, *a bird in the hand is better than two in the bush*, a simple expression of this notoriety? Now, if a sum currently owned is worth more, is more useful, is preferable to the assurance of receiving a similar sum in one or several years' time, it is not true that the lender receives as much as he gives when he does not stipulate interest, for he gives the money and only receives an assurance. Now, if he receives less, why should this difference not be compensated by the assurance of an increase in the sum proportioned to the delay? This compensation is precisely the rate of interest.[12]

Although Turgot understood that the premium of the present is bound up with the distinction between sooner and later, his statement of time preference is inferior to Menger's. It fails to trace the source of the premium back completely to a preference for a given satisfaction sooner instead of later and instead stops the logical chain one link short with the good in which time

---

[11] Menger, *Principles of Economics*, p. 161. Italics in original. As discussed below, by "the value of the services of capital" Menger meant that possessing capital advances a person in time toward the attainment of his end.

[12] A.R.J. Turgot, "Mémoire sur les prêts d'argent," quoted in Peter D. Groenewegen, "A Reinterpretation of Turgot's Theory of Capital and Interest," *The Economic Journal* 81, no. 322 (June, 1971): 330. Italics in original.

preference is expressed, i.e., money. Menger supplied the missing link. The premium of present money over future money is caused by the preference people have for a satisfaction sooner instead of later.

In addition to seeing that the premium is bound up with the distinction between sooner and later, Turgot also saw that the premium was expressed across the opportunities to use money to invest in different lines of productive activity. In analyzing how leather production would get started, he wrote:

> It must then be one of those proprietors of capitals, or moveable accumulated property that must employ them, supplying them with advances in part for the construction and purchase of materials, and partly for the daily salaries of the workmen that are preparing them. It is he that must expect the sale of the leather, which is to return him not only his advances, but also an emolument sufficient to indemnify him for what his money would have procured him, had he turned it to the acquisition of lands, and moreover of the salary due to his troubles and care, to his risqué, and even to his skill; for surely, upon equal profits, he would have preferred living without solicitude, on the revenue of the land, which he could have purchased with the same capital.[13]

The consideration of interest as a payment for advancing capital funding necessary for production processes is no different for agriculture than for manufacturing. Turgot wrote:

> It is the proprietors of great capitals, who, in order to make them productive in undertakings of agriculture, take leases of lands, and pay to the owners large rents, taking on themselves the whole burthen of advances. Their case must necessarily be the same as that of the undertakers of manufacturers. Like them, they are obliged to make the first advances toward the undertaking.... Like them, they ought to have not only their capital, I mean, all their prior and annual advances returned,

---

13 A.R.J. Turgot, *Reflections on the Formation and Distribution of Wealth* (London: E. Spragg, 1793 [1774]), Rfl. 135, §60.

but, 1st, a profit equal to the revenue they could have acquired with their capital, exclusive of any fatigue; 2nd, the salary, and the price of their own trouble and industry; 3rd, an emolument to enable them to replace the effects employed in their enterprise...[14]

The interest return for advancing capital in any line of production, for Turgot, was the same as that for advancing capital outside of production (without fatigue or labor), i.e., a loan contract. The reason for this result is that the same trade of present money for future money occurs in both cases and present money always commands a premium over future money regardless of other circumstances.

Turgot also understood capitalization. He wrote, "Whoever, either by the revenue of his land, or by the salary of his labour or industry, receives every year a higher income than he needs to spend, may lay up the residue and accumulate it: these accumulated values are what we name a capital."[15] A person may dissipate his capital by spending in excess of his income or he may invest it. If he does the latter, the present price he pays for an asset, Turgot argued, is the sum of its future revenue. He wrote:

> The [person who invests his capital] can draw a far greater advantage from it [than he who spends it]; for an estate in land of a certain revenue, being by an equivalent of a sum of value equal to the [annual] revenue, taken a certain number of times [for the number of years it is generated], it follows, that any sum whatsoever of value is equivalent to an estate in land, producing a revenue equal to a fixed proportion of that sum. It is perfectly the same whether the amount of this capital consists in a mass of metal, or any other matter, since money represents all kinds of value, as well as all kinds of value represent money. By these means the possessor of a capital may at first employ it in the purchase of lands; but he is not without other resources.[16]

---

14 Turgot, *Reflections*, Rfl. 138, §62.
15 Ibid., Rfl. 130, §58.
16 Ibid. The additions in brackets are explained by Turgot in the previous paragraph (§57) in which he is dealing with land value in an economy without

Competitive bidding for assets, according to Turgot, still leaves a discount for time preference. He wrote:

> The competition between rich undertakers of cultivation fixes the current price of leases, in proportion to the fertility of the soil, and of the rate at which its productions are sold, always according to the calculation which farmers make both of their expenditures, and of the profits they ought to draw from their advances.[17]

Böhm-Bawerk Against the PTPT

Although Eugen von Böhm-Bawerk is often cited as a champion of the time preference view of interest for his exhaustive work in demolishing other theories of interest, he clearly rejected the PTPT. In the first lines of his *History and Critique of Interest Theories* he states what he considers to be the problem of interest: "Whoever is the owner of a capital sum is ordinarily able to derive from it a permanent net income which goes under the scientific name of interest in the broad sense of the term." As Böhm-Bawerk makes clear in describing his theory, however, this way of putting the matter allows for both time preference and value productivity influences on interest. He wrote, "And so the phenomenon of interest presents, on the whole, the remarkable picture of a lifeless thing, capital, producing an everlasting and inexhaustible supply of goods."[18] The PTPT, in contrast, makes no claim about the amount of goods being generated in production, but only about the net (monetary) income earned from trading present money for future money. It states that time preference will always generate a positive difference between the selling prices of output and the buying prices of inputs. It matters not whether the supply of goods is increasing, stagnant, or decreasing. Fetter

---

money. In the paragraph quoted, he introduces money and thus, capital and capitalization. In §58, he deals with the capital value of land and in §59 he moves on to the capital value of assets in manufacturing or industry.
17 Turgot, *Reflections*, Rfl. 140, §63.
18 Eugen von Böhm-Bawerk, *History and Critique of Interest Theories* (Spring Mills, Penn.: Libertarian Press, 1959 [1884]), p. 1.

wrote, "The interest-rate is but an index of the ratio inherent in the equilibrium of psychological forces, desires for present and future incomes; that is, time preference."[19]

Although Böhm-Bawerk constructed the theory of the capital structure within Menger's system, which was a necessary step between the views of Turgot and Menger and the PTPT of Fetter, he failed to appreciate the straightforward conclusions drawn from discounting and capitalization by Turgot and Menger. He mischaracterized Turgot's theory as a fructification theory of interest. Starting with the assertion that Turgot was "the greatest of the physiocrats," Böhm-Bawerk claimed that Turgot grounded interest in the return to land. According to Böhm-Bawerk, Turgot argued that "land guarantees a permanent income without labor."[20] He wrote:

> Since in this way the owner of capital can make it yield a permanent yearly income by buying land with it, he will not be inclined to invest his capital in an industrial, agricultural, or commercial enterprise, unless he can expect just as large a net return as he could obtain through the purchase of land over and above the reimbursement of his expense and compensation for his trouble. On that account capital, in all these branches of employment, *must* yield an income.[21]

Originary interest is this income stream. Moreover, "The entrepreneur without capital is gladly willing," Böhm-Bawerk wrote, "to pay to the man who entrusts him with a capital some part of the gain which the borrowed capital yields." In this way, contract interest arises. In either case, interest is an opportunity cost of land rent and hence, Böhm-Bawerk's characterization of Turgot's theory as a "fructification theory of interest."[22]

As we have seen, however, Turgot argued that the advances of capital funding necessary for setting in motion any production

---

19 Frank Fetter, *Economic Principles* (New York: The Century Co., 1915), p. 313.
20 Böhm-Bawerk, *History and Critique*, p. 40.
21 Ibid., p. 41. Italics in original.
22 Ibid.

process commands interest because people prefer present money to future money. For Turgot, this is true of investments in land as well as in other assets. Competitive bidding among entrepreneurs for assets bids their prices up to the sum of the anticipated revenue stream discounted by time preference, therefore, interest is earned in production as well as contract loans.

Likewise, Böhm-Bawerk's critique of Menger's theory of interest misses the mark. He seized upon Menger's phrase "command over the services of capital" to label his theory a Use Theory. According to Böhm-Bawerk use theorists claim that interest is compensation for a separate use of capital not included in its productivity and hence, its price. Böhm-Bawerk is not so bold as to lump Menger in with other use theorists, particularly in those in what he labels the Say-Hermann tradition. He recognizes Menger's distinctive claims and gives his theory separate treatment.[23] Menger first demonstrates that the value of higher order goods derives from the anticipated value of lower order goods that they will produce in the future and not the value of lower order goods that exist in the present. Then, he claims that the surplus value of capital must be related to the time necessary to use higher order goods in the present to produce lower order goods in the future. Menger wrote:

> In order to transform goods of higher order into goods of lower order, the passage of a certain period of time is necessary. Hence, whenever economic goods are to be produced, *command of the services of capital is necessary for a certain period of time.*
>
> ... In order to have a good or a quantity of goods of lower order at our command at a future time, it is not sufficient to have fleeting possession of the corresponding goods of higher order at some single point in time, but instead necessary that we retain command of these goods of higher order for a period of time that varies in length according to the nature of the particular process of production, and that we *fix* them in this production process of the duration of that period.

---

23 Böhm-Bawerk, *History and Critique*, pp. 141–77.

> ... [C]ommand of quantities of economic goods for given periods of time has value to economizing men, just as other economic goods have value to them. From this it follows that the aggregate present value of all the goods of higher order necessary for the production of a good of lower order can be set equal to the prospective value of the product to economizing men only if the value of the services of capital during the production period is included.[24]

Böhm-Bawerk takes this to mean that Menger is asserting that "command" over the services of capital is a use value of capital separate from its productivity. Menger, however, used the concept of "command" over something as a requisite for it to be a good. The fourth property something must have to acquire "goods-character," is "command of the thing sufficient to direct it to the satisfaction of the need," Menger wrote.[25] In referring to the definition of the term "capital," Menger is merely applying the requisites of a good to it. He wrote, "the time period during which an economizing individual has command of the necessary quantities of economic goods must be long enough to permit a production process (in the economic sense of the term) to take place."[26] In other words, "command over the services of capital" refers to the period of time during which a person has command of the productivity of capital. Menger gave the following example:

> Suppose, for example, we wish to determine the value of the goods of higher order that assure us command of a given quantity of grain a year hence. The value of the seed grain, the services of land, the specialized agricultural labor services, and all the other goods of higher order necessary for the production of the given quantity of grain will indeed be equal to the *prospective* value of the grain at the end of the year, but only on condition that the value of a year's command of these economic

---

24 Menger, *Principles of Economics*, pp. 157–58. Italics in original.
25 Ibid., p. 52.
26 Ibid., pp. 303–04.

goods to the economizing individuals concerned is included in the sum. The *present* value of these goods of higher order by themselves is therefore equal to the value of the prospective product minus the value of the services of the capital employed.[27]

Since Menger likens the surplus to discounting, it's more likely the phrase "value of a year's command of these economic goods" refers to the time involved in production rather than a use value of the goods separate from their productivity. Command of these economic goods for a year advances a person toward the attainment of his end while command of these goods for only a fraction of the time necessary for production would not advance him toward his production goal. Instead, the person would have to start anew after securing a year's command of the necessary production goods. Murray Rothbard makes a similar claim in saying that the (net) service of capital is advancing a person in time toward his goal. Rothbard wrote:

> What does earn an income is the conversion of future goods into present goods; because of the universal fact of time preference, future satisfactions are always at a discount compared to present satisfactions. The *owning* and holding of capital goods from date one, when factor services are purchased, until the product is sold at date two is what capitalist investors accomplish.... In other words, capital goods have been advanced from an earlier, *more distantly future* stage, to a later or *less distantly future* stage. The time for this transformation will be covered by a rate of time preference....
>
> The capitalists' function is thus a *time* function, and their income is precisely an income representing the agio of present as compared to future goods. This interest income, then is *not* derived from the concrete, heterogeneous capital *goods*, but from the generalized investment of time.[28]

---

27 Menger, *Principles of Economics*, p. 158. Italics in original.
28 Murray Rothbard, *Man, Economy, and State with Power and Market*, scholar's edition (Auburn, Ala.: Ludwig von Mises Institute, 2004), pp. 373–74. Italics in original.

Here is Menger's own summary of the section of *Principles of Economics* devoted to the value of complementary quantities of goods of higher order:

> The aggregate present value of all the complementary quantities of goods of higher order ... necessary for the production of a good of lower or first order is equal to the prospective value of the product. But it is necessary to include in the sum not only the goods of higher order technically required for its production but also the services of capital and the activity of the entrepreneur. For these are as unavoidably necessary in every economic production of goods as the technical requisites already mentioned. Hence the *present* value of the technical factors of production by themselves is not equal to the full prospective value of the product, but always behaves in such a way that a margin for the value of the services of capital and entrepreneurial activity remains.[29]

Böhm-Bawerk's Theory of Interest

Of all his predecessors on interest theory, Böhm-Bawerk gave pride of place to John Rae. Böhm-Bawerk thought so highly of Rae's ideas that having discovered and read his *Statement of Some New Principles on the Subject of Political Economy* after publishing the first edition of *History and Critique*, he included in the second edition an additional chapter presenting and critiquing Rae's views. About him, Böhm-Bawerk wrote, "It was on the subject of the theory of capital, more specifically, that Rae held a number of exceedingly original and remarkable views, and those views exhibit unmistakable similarity to views which were developed about a half century later by Jevons and myself."[30] In contrasting Rae to Turgot, Böhm-Bawerk wrote:

> [Rae's] line of reasoning contains a great and an original step forward, in comparison with several attempts found in earlier writings. As we know, Galiani and Turgot had already

---

29 Menger, *Principles of Economics*, p. 161. Italics in original.
30 Böhm-Bawerk, *History and Critique*, p. 208.

coined occasional catch-phrases which hinted at a connection between interest and a difference in the estimation of present and future goods. However, they did not develop the idea nor even adhere to it.[31]

Rae understood time preference differently than Menger. For him, it was the premium on present goods over future goods. "There is no man perhaps, to whom a good to be enjoyed to day [sic]," he wrote, "would not seem of very different importance, from one exactly similar to be enjoyed twelve years hence, even though the arrival of both were equally certain."[32] Böhm-Bawerk, as we will see, adopted Rae's view over that of Menger.

The main use Rae made of his concept of time preference was to explain intertemporal allocation of goods. Time preference determines the extent to which people are willing to accumulate capital by trading present goods for future goods. Capital accumulation would proceed apace were it not for human weaknesses, both mental and physical. Take away man's frailties and "a pleasure to be enjoyed, or a pain to be endured, fifty or a hundred years hence, would be considered deserving the same attention as if it were to befall us fifty or a hundred minutes hence," Rae wrote, "and the sacrifice of a smaller present good, for a greater future good, would be readily made, to whatever period that futurity might extend." Unfortunately, man has time preference because, "life, and the power to enjoy it, are the most uncertain of all things, and we are not guided altogether by reason."[33]

Given the weakness of the human condition, Rae concluded, "A mere reasonable regard to their own interest, would, therefore, place the present very far above the future, in the estimation of most men." Like Böhm-Bawerk, Rae claimed that there were several psychological reasons for preferring the present. In addition to human frailty, Rae asserted that another such reason is

---

31 Böhm-Bawerk, *History and Critique*, pp. 225–26.
32 John Rae, *Statement of Some New Principles on the Subject of Political Economy* (Boston: Hilliard, Gray, and Co., 1834), p. 120.
33 Ibid., p. 119.

the "lively conception of enjoyments" men have for "the immediate object of desire" over the "dull and dubious" prospects of a future good.[34] These psychological tendencies for present goods, according to Rae are balanced against other psychological tendencies for future goods. What he calls "the social and benevolent affections" and "reasoning and reflective habits" both "urge the propriety of providing for [the future]."[35] Men's willingness to forego present goods to acquire future ones, for Rae, is determined by the balance of these psychological tendencies. With people's "effective desire of accumulation" determined by this balance of psychological factors, the amount of capital accumulation is determined by the available physically more productive production processes.[36]

Time preference not only influences people's "effective desire to accumulate" and thereby, the extent of capital accumulation, it also affects the allocation of their investment into different lines of capital goods or "particular orders of instruments." Rae argued that time preference would lead investors to adopt production processes that generate their returns more quickly. "By rapidly exhausting the capacity of any instrument," Rae wrote, "the returns yielded by it are not lessened, but quickened."[37] With a given "effective desire of accumulation" people would produce the array of capital goods across the different lines of production that yield the same physical surplus most quickly. For example, if machine tools double output in two years while assembly line equipment doubles output in one year and an investor is limited by his time preference to invest in just one line, then he will choose the line that generates its surplus most quickly, i.e., assembly line equipment.[38] Physical ratios of the "particular orders of instruments" can be ranked from most to least productive lines and investment will be allocated into the

---

34 Rae, *Subject of Political Economy*, p. 120.
35 Ibid., p. 122.
36 Ibid., p. 129.
37 Ibid., p. 164. See his example of tree cutting, p. 172.
38 Ibid., p. 172.

most productive lines to the point where the "effective desire to accumulate" is exhausted. Any change in the physical ratios will set in motion a readjustment of the stock of capital until the lines of production are brought into conformity again with the "effective desire of accumulation."[39] When the ratios are expressed in a numeraire money then there will emerge a general rate of return on capital paid to producers according to the average length of the periods of production in the economy.[40] Commodity money is not essential to this process. It merely measures the stock of capital in the same fashion as any numeraire money can do. Interest is expressed in commodity money only because it, and not a numeraire money, is the medium of exchange. What interest refers to is the physical ratio of the "orders of instruments" brought about by the "effective desire of accumulation." Money merely simplifies and standardizes the physical ratios.[41]

Even though there is no production underlying credit markets, the rates of interest in these markets will conform to the underlying physical ratios of the "orders of instruments."[42] Rae argued that the premium of the present had to be paid whether the exchange was for present capital goods in production or for present money in credit markets and that the payment in money would be equivalent in the two cases.[43]

In summing up, Rae wrote, "We may then assume that rate of interest as a fair measure of the real average rate of profits, in any country, and consequently of the order in our series, at which instruments are there arrived."[44]

Böhm-Bawerk could only muster two major criticisms of Rae's views. First, he took Rae to task for holding to an incorrect theory of pricing, as Rae saw labor effort as the measure of the value of things. Böhm-Bawerk called his price theory "a theory of

---

39 Rae, *Subject of Political Economy*, pp. 172–73.
40 Ibid., pp. 174–75
41 Ibid., pp. 193–95.
42 Ibid., p. 194.
43 Ibid., p. 195.
44 Ibid., p. 196.

replacement costs."[45] Without a marginal utility theory of price, Rae claimed a direct relationship between changes in physical productivity and changes in price spreads. Because of this error, Rae lapses into a productivity view of interest.[46] In this criticism, Böhm-Bawerk exposes what he considers to be a key issue for any theory of interest. He wrote:

> The difficulty is—and indeed, I think it is at once the greatest and the most stimulating difficulty of the whole problem of interest—the difficulty is, to explain in what manner, and by the employment of what intermediary processes those heterogeneous component elements (they include objective technical factors, and highly subjective psychological motives) combine and cooperate to produce that end result which we know as the homogeneous phenomenon of interest.[47]

As we have seen above, the causal-realist approach argues that all factors affecting human action and choice have their effects determined by judgments of the human mind. Only the PTPT applies this insight fully to the theory of interest. Not only Rae, but Böhm-Bawerk himself, as we will see below, fails to do so.

The second main weakness of Rae's account of interest according to Böhm-Bawerk was that he set up technical factors as a second line alongside psychological factors in determining the rate of interest. What led him astray is that he "took for granted … that a mere physical increase in production is identical with an increase excess in value over the costs of production," according to Böhm-Bawerk, and thus, "interpreted considerations which can explain only an increase in production, as an adequate explanation of the phenomena of surplus and interest."[48] Consider a technological improvement that renders greater output with given inputs. According to Rae, the introduction of such an

---

45 Böhm-Bawerk, *History and Critique*, p. 218.
46 Ibid., pp. 230f.
47 Ibid., p. 227.
48 Ibid., p. 228.

improvement, given the "effective desire to accumulate," would lead people to give up the lowest productive orders in order to invest in the new, higher productive orders. Doing so, however, raises the rate of return. Böhm-Bawerk chides Rae for conflating physical returns with value returns, rightly protesting that prices would adjust to normalize the exchange value surplus or rate of return, in the technically more productive processes. Rae could hardly have arrived at this correct result since he lacked "the modern theory of marginal utility."[49]

Armed with the marginal utility theory of price, Böhm-Bawerk develops his theory of interest from Rae's insights. Like Rae, Böhm-Bawerk claims that the preference for present over future goods is merely a tendency brought about by several complementary causes. He gives examples of a future good of "equal quality and quantity" compared to a present good being either more or less highly valued. Present food being more highly valued by citizens of a besieged fortress than future food a year after the siege. In the winter, by contrast, ice is valued less highly in the present than ice in the summer, six months into the future.[50] He thought, however, that "present goods have in general greater subjective value than future (and intermediate) goods of equal quantity and quality.... This result is the fruit of the collaboration of a number of causes which, individually, differ markedly but which, it just so happens, exert their influence in the same direction."[51]

Böhm-Bawerk's three causes are as follows. First, "if a person suffers in the present from appreciable lack of certain goods, or of goods in general, but has reason to hope to be more generously provided for at a future time, then that person will always place a higher value on a given quantity of immediately available goods than on the same quantity of future goods."[52] Moreover,

---

49 Böhm-Bawerk, *History and Critique*, pp. 232–37.
50 Eugen von Böhm-Bawerk, *Positive Theory of Interest* (Spring Mills, Penn.: Libertarian Press, 1959 [1889]), p. 263.
51 Ibid., p. 265.
52 Ibid., p. 266.

if a person believes the present is more amply supplied than the future, he may still value present goods over future goods. This is because present goods, that can be stored for the future, render any one of the most valuable possibilities for action at each moment from the present into the future while future goods render only the most valuable possibility at the future moment when they are available. Present goods, that can be stored, must have at least the same value as future goods since they can be used for any of the most valuable courses of action from the present to the future, including the most valuable course of action for the future goods. Whatever the merits of this cause it refers to psychology and not to pure time preference, the preference for a satisfaction sooner instead of the same satisfaction later.

Second, "we systematically undervalue our future wants and also the means which serve to satisfy them."[53] Although Böhm-Bawerk asserts that "psychologists would appear to be more competent than we economists are" to explain this fact, he asserts the following three reasons.[54] "There are, then, three contributory or partial causes for the lesser valuation of future utility; (a) erroneous valuation by reason of the fragmentary imagery of future wants; (b) lack of will power and (c) consideration of the uncertainty of life."[55] Like the first cause, this second cause is psychological and, therefore, does not refer to pure time preference.

Third, "as a general rule, present goods are for technological reasons preferable means to the satisfaction of wants and for that reason they are a warranty of higher marginal utility than are future goods."[56] This occurs because present goods permit a person a longer period of production to any given date in the future than future goods do and longer periods of production are more productive. And "for one and the same person at one and the same point of time, the larger quantity always has

---

53 Böhm-Bawerk, *Positive Theory of Interest*, p. 268.
54 Ibid., p. 269.
55 Ibid., p. 271.
56 Ibid., p. 273.

the greater value."⁵⁷ This cause, too, does not refer to pure time preference.

Böhm-Bawerk goes on to demonstrate that "the superiority in value of present means of production, which is based on their technological superiority, is not something borrowed from the other two factors but rather something that would arise spontaneously even if those two factors were not operative at all."⁵⁸ Moreover, it doesn't work through subject factors, but combines with them as a cooperating independent factor to produce the overall effect.

Böhm-Bawerk goes on to show that the third factor operates for consumer goods as well as producer goods and therefore, the third cause is universal. The reason is that possession of present consumer goods provides for a person's subsistence and thereby, permits him to produce capital goods and set down the road to longer, more productive processes. Possessing future consumer goods leaves present consumption unmet and therefore, requires a person to devote producer goods to making consumer goods via shorter, less productive production processes.⁵⁹

Böhm-Bawerk then argues that the superiority in value of present goods over future goods "is also brought about through the fact that when durable types of consumer goods are produced, their durability and hence the quantity of their renditions of service often augments at a more rapid rate than do the necessary expenditures required for their production." It follows that production of durable goods renders more services per unit of labor used in production. Moreover, more time must elapse between producing a more durable good and the enjoyment of all its services than that necessary to enjoy all of the services of a less durable good. And this is "a completely analogous reason for a superiority in value of present over future goods based on their technical superiority."⁶⁰

---

57 Böhm-Bawerk, *Positive Theory of Interest*, p. 275.
58 Ibid., p. 279.
59 Ibid., p. 280.
60 Ibid., p. 282.

On the key issue of how the different causal factors interrelate to determine the rate of interest, Böhm-Bawerk claimed that the relationship among the three causes of interest is cumulative between the two subjective factors and alternative between the subject factors and the productivity factor. Interest is determined by whichever one, the subjective pair or productivity, brings about the greater premium of present over future goods. A greater premium will always be chosen over a lesser one and thus, be realized in action. Moreover, neither the subjective factors nor the productivity factor can augment the other in determining the premium of the present over the future. If the productivity factor renders the larger premium, then the subjective factors cannot augment it because it affects all productive uses of present producer goods to the same extent and thereby leaves their relative positions exactly the same. If the subjective factors, inadequate present provision and undervaluation of the future, render the larger premium, then the productivity factor cannot augment it because present uses will be chosen over longer, more productive processes. Because the subjective factors alternate with the productivity factor, one of them is always in play causing a premium of the present.[61]

Fetter in Defense of the PTPT

Fetter's reaction was critical. On Böhm-Bawerk's key question, Fetter wrote, "There is a relation between roundaboutness and time-preference, but it is one in which the mere mechanical method is passive and subordinate to human choice, time preference."[62] Discounting and capitalization undermine Böhm-Bawerk's claim that more capital, in value terms, implies longer processes of production and therefore lower interest rates. With a physical concept of capital, there is no way to aggregate capital goods to determine whether more or less capital is used in any production process that is more roundabout. With a value

---

61 Böhm-Bawerk, *Positive Theory of Interest*, pp. 284–85.
62 Fetter, *Economic Principles*, p. 261.

concept of capital, "the argument contains the fallacy of the vicious circle," Fetter wrote, because the interest rate must be known in order to calculate the value of capital.[63] Because Irving Fisher accepted his view of capitalization, Fetter presumed that Fisher sided with him in the capitalization argument against Böhm-Bawerk.[64] This misapprehension led Fetter to consider, temporarily, Fisher a pure time preference theorist, a view he corrected in "Interest Theories New and Old." In summarizing his view of Böhm-Bawerk's theory, Fetter wrote:

> Böhm-Bawerk as a disciple of Menger sought to make the theory of capital his peculiar domain, but after beginnings which pointed toward a value investment concept and after painstaking studies of earlier views he adopted the conventional confused concept of "capital in general" as "a group of [physical] products which serve as means to the acquisition of goods." This foredoomed him to a productivity theory of interest—the very thing he had attempted to avoid.[65]

If Fetter's capitalization argument is sufficient to expose the error in Böhm-Bawerk's position it is a more than sufficient critique of the eclectic view of Rae. Böhm-Bawerk himself criticized Rae for having two independent lines of determinates of the rate of interest, time preference on the one hand and physical productivity on the other and thereby, failing to give an adequate answer to his key question about interest rate theories: what is the relationship between the subjective and objective factors that influence the interest rate? Böhm-Bawerk held that both the subjective and objective factors affect time preference, defined as the preference people have for present goods over future goods and

---

[63] Frank Fetter, "The 'Roundabout Process' in the Interest Theory," *Quarterly Journal of Economics* 17 (November, 1902); reprinted in Fetter, *Capital, Interest, and Rent*, Murray N. Rothbard, ed. (Kansas City: Sheed Andrews and McMeel, 1977), p. 177. Böhm-Bawerk's response to Fetter's argument is in *Further Essays on Capital and Interest* (Spring Mills, Penn.: Libertarian Press, 1959 [1909–1912]), pp. 68–71.

[64] Irving Fisher, *The Rate of Interest* (New York: Macmillan Company, 1907), pp. 225–27.

[65] Frank Fetter, "Capital," in *Encyclopedia of the Social Sciences* 3 (New York: Macmillan, 1930–1935); reprinted in Fetter, *Capital, Interest, and Rent*, pp. 146–47.

therefore, affect the rate of interest defined as the price spread between present goods and future goods. Fetter's view is even stricter, ruling out not only physical productivity from influencing interest rates (as Rae claimed) but also the value of physical productivity (as Böhm-Bawerk claimed). Following Menger, pure time preference, for Fetter, is the preference people have for a given satisfaction sooner instead of the same satisfaction later. The rate of interest, reflecting pure time preference, emerges in the exchange of present money for future money. The prices of inputs are determined by the rate of interest through capitalization of the revenues generated by their productivity. The value productivity of capital may affect which present goods are traded for which future goods, but not the pure rate of time preference. Both Böhm-Bawerk's and Fetter's critiques would apply to any eclectic theory of interest, including the neoclassical view that the rate of interest is jointly determined by the productivity of investment possibilities curve and time preference indifference curves.[66]

When Fetter published "Interest Rate Theories Old and New" in 1914, he expressed exasperation that the battles fought, and seemingly won, for the PTPT a decade earlier had not won the war. The apparent recantation of such a prominent proponent of the theory as Fisher was cause for alarm and even dismay for the prospects of victory for the PTPT, and by implication, for the causal-realist approach. Fetter was bemused that economists were turning toward an eclectic explanation for interest relying on impatience and productivity. The source of retrogression was the failure to fully integrate the theory of prices of consumer goods with the theory of prices for producer goods. It is futile to assert that costs of production are an independent causal factor, alongside consumer preferences, in determining the prices of consumer goods once one perceives that rental prices for producer goods are, themselves, determined by consumer

---

66 Hayek held such an eclectic view of interest. See F.A. Hayek, "Time Preferences and Productivity: A Reconsideration," *Economica*, n.s., 12, no. 45 (February, 1945): 22–25.

preferences through their causal power over entrepreneurial demand to rent producer goods.

Likewise, it is futile to assert that technical productivity is an independent cause of interest rates once one perceives that purchase prices, or capital values, of producer goods are determined by consumer preferences through entrepreneurial demand to purchase producer goods outright. Such a complete integration disposes of productivity causal explanations seemingly more sophisticated than their naïve counterparts demolished by Böhm-Bawerk.

As Fetter makes clear, a fully integrated theory rules out "opportunity cost" arguments, common among authors of eclectic theories, to reconcile the eclectic factors into a unified system, i.e., to answer Böhm-Bawerk's key question: how do the different causal factors come together to produce a uniform rate of interest. Fetter wrote:

> The value of land usually is explained simply as the capitalizing of its rents at "the prevailing rate of interest." The rate is assumed to be fixed by conditions in manufacturing and commerce, and if five percent can be gotten there the capitalist would never buy land unless investment in it were made equally attractive. The cause of the rate thus is supposed to rest outside the transaction itself, the exchange of land for other capital seeking investment. The economic student is safe in assuming always that explanations of this sort are fallacious. The cause of value in any one exchange or any one industry is not thus to be juggled and shifted into another industry. It is true that the values of goods are so wonderfully interrelated by substitution that as the price of fresh beef will affect that of salt mackerel, so the capitalization rate of machinery affects that of land; but the influence is not from one side only, it is mutual. When anything has value, it must have in itself an independent cause of value.[67]

Although Fetter mistook Fisher for a PTPT advocate, Fisher was an unwavering follower of Rae and Böhm-Bawerk. He

---

67 Fetter, *Principles of Economics*, pp. 124–25.

dedicated his books, *The Rate of Interest*, published in 1907, "To the memory of John Rae who laid the foundations upon which I have endeavored to build" and *The Theory of Interest*, published in 1930, "To the memory of John Rae and Eugen von Böhm-Bawerk, who laid the foundations upon which I have endeavored to build."[68] Seemingly with Fetter in mind, Fisher made it clear in *The Theory of Interest* that he had always sided with Rae and Böhm-Bawerk. He wrote:

> I have considered the criticisms of the former book which have come to my notice, and have, as a consequence, modified the form of presentation materially. Though, in substance, my theory of interest has been altered scarcely at all, its exposition has been so amplified and recast that it will, I anticipate, seem, to those who misunderstood my first book, more changed than it seems to me.[69]

The substance of Fisher's theory is the same as that of Rae's. He wrote:

> Years after *The Rate of Interest* was published, I suggested the more popular terms "impatience" in place of "agio" or "time preference." This catchword has been widely adopted, and, to my surprise, has led to a widespread but false impression that I had overlooked or neglected the productivity or investment opportunity side entirely. Every essential part of [my theory] was at least foreshadowed by John Rae in 1834.[70]

In *The Rate of Interest*, Fisher lauds Böhm-Bawerk for perfecting the theory of Rae, except in his third cause of a preference for present goods over future goods. He wrote:

> Böhm-Bawerk has presented the agio theory clearly and forcibly, and had disentangled it from the crude and incorrect notions with which it had previously been associated. It is only when he attempts to add to it his special feature of a

---

68 Fisher, *The Rate of Interest*, and Irving Fisher, *The Theory of Interest* (New York: Macmillan Co., 1930).
69 Fisher, *Theory of Interest*, p. 4.
70 Ibid., pp. 6–7.

"technical superiority of present over future goods" that he has impaired rather than improved it.[71]

It is from the preference for the early over the late fruition of *any* productive process that the so-called "technical superiority of present over future goods" derives all its force. The imagined "third circumstance" producing a superiority in present goods is only the first two circumstances in disguise.[72]

In contrast to Fetter's argument against Böhm-Bawerk, that capitalization subsumes the greater productivity of roundabout methods of production and thus exposes interest as an effect of pure time preference, Fisher agrees with Fetter that such technical superiority has no independent effect on interest, but claims that it works by animating the first two causes of the superiority of present goods over future goods. Contrary to Böhm-Bawerk's claim, Fisher argued that the third cause is not alternative to the subjective causes. He wrote:

> The essential fact is that its [the technical superiority of present goods] presence does not produce interest when the other two [underestimation of the future and under-endowment of the present] are absent. In short, the "technical superiority" of present goods is a delusion, and the only way in which the existence of long processes of production acts on interest is by overendowing [sic] the future and underendowing the present, thus creating a "scarcity value" of present goods.[73]

> If we cast out from the agio theory Böhm-Bawerk's special feature, his alleged "technical superiority of present goods," the theory which remains is believed to be correct. It is, however, still incomplete, for there remains the gap which Böhm-Bawerk sought to fill,—the formulation of the exact manner in which the "technique" or actual conditions of production enter into the determination of interest. In Part III we shall attempt to supply this deficiency.[74]

---

71 Fisher, *Rate of Interest*, pp. 53–54.
72 Ibid., p. 71. Italics in original.
73 Ibid., p. 72.
74 Ibid., p. 74.

Despite their differences, both Fisher and Böhm-Bawerk assert that time preference refers to the trade-off between present goods and future goods. Fetter, in contrast, says that pure time preference is the difference in value of a given satisfaction obtained sooner instead of later. It originates not from a laundry list of subjective and objective considerations playing against each other to yield a net premium on present goods over future goods, but from the temporal character of human existence. Pure time preference, Fetter wrote, is the "preference for the present unit simply because it *is* present."[75]

Fetter on the PTPT

In his *Principles of Economics*, Fetter constructs economic theory in the causal-realist style, starting with the nature of man and the world and deducing laws of economics from them. From the existence of both human wants and objects capable of satisfying these wants, Fetter defines the concept of wealth as "the collective term for those things which are felt to be related to the gratification of wants."[76] Wants recur and goods deteriorate and thus, a succession of goods is required to more fully satisfy human wants. The succession of goods renders psychic income. "The value of consumption goods is derived from the pleasurable psychic impressions which they aid to produce," Fetter wrote, "and these psychic effects constitute the psychic income."[77] Fetter then develops the theory of direct exchange and barter prices and the crucial concept of rent. "The essential thought in rent," Fetter wrote, "is that it is the value of the usufruct as distinguished from the value of the use-bearer or thing itself."[78] Fetter, then, explains the relationship between wealth and rent. He wrote:

---

[75] Fetter, *Economic Principles*, p. 249. Italics in original.
[76] Fetter, *Principles of Economics*, p. 17.
[77] Ibid., p. 43.
[78] Ibid., p. 55.

> Gratification, afforded directly or indirectly, is the basis of all values. The relation of most kinds of wealth to wants is indirect; but gratification thus afforded indirectly is none the less the basis on which the usufruct of wealth is estimated. Men find the logical or causal connection between direct goods, or final product, and indirect goods, or agents.
>
> To explain the value of the durable wealth, or rent-bearer, a still farther step in thought must be taken. The value of the rent-bearer is based on the series of rents which it affords. To explain how these rents are added to give the value of the indirect agents is the task of a theory of capitalization.[79]

As Fetter realized, the prerequisite to a theory of capitalization is money. He begins the third major division of his book, "Capitalization and Time-Value," developing the nature and origin of money in the Mengerian tradition, moves on to explaining money prices, the concept of capital, and then capitalization of rent, and with it, interest. "Capital to-day," Fetter wrote, "may be defined as economic wealth expressed in terms of the general unit of value."[80] A capitalist economy is one in which wealth has been capitalized. Fetter wrote:

> As here presented, the essence of the capital concept is in the mode or form of expression of wealth, not in the physical nature, the origin of its value, or any peculiarity in the kind of wealth; the content of the concept is limited only by man's thought of wealth, every good becoming capital when it is capitalized, that is, when the totality of its uses is expressed as a present sum of values.[81]

For capitalization to be possible, rents must be in monetary form, i.e., it must be possible to buy and sell successions of monetary rents. As Fetter points out, trade of successions of rents was an important form of raising capital funding in the Middle Ages. It did not fall under the usury restrictions of the church

---

79 Fetter, *Principles of Economics*, p. 73.
80 Ibid., p. 115.
81 Ibid., p. 116.

even though it involved implicit interest payments, i.e., the capital fund expended was less than the sum of the succession of rents received.[82]

Only at this stage of the development of economic theory does Fetter introduce interest. Like rent and capital, interest can only be expressed in money. Fetter wrote:

> In the interest contract for the loan of capital the interest always is and must be expressed in money; the capital sum must be expressed as value; and the interest rate expresses the relation between these two values. In each of these features the interest contract is in contrast with the renting contract."[83]

Fetter goes on to explain that capitalization creates a uniform treatment of any stream of future payments, regardless of its source. Whether the payments come from the rent of land, the net income of production, loan contracts, etc. capitalization of the assets ensures a uniform rate of interest.[84] Summing up, Fetter wrote, "When we have reached this point in the reasoning, our proposition must suggest itself as self-evidently true in this form: the value of any good is the sum of the entire series of rents it contains, discounted, at *some* rate, to their present worth."[85]

On the relationship between capital, rent, and interest, Fetter wrote:

> Rent, or income, is a link in the chain of value, connecting gratification or psychic income, consumption goods, rent or usufruct value, and finally capital value. To one keeping in mind the logical cause of value, it becomes inconceivable that capital value could precede income, a view possible only when a fragment of the problem is seen. This being true, the mere mention of a capital sum implies the interest problem, and assumes the interest rate. The capital is of that amount because the anticipated incomes, discounted at some rate, equal that sum.[86]

---

82 Fetter, *Principles of Economics*, pp. 118–20.
83 Ibid., p. 116.
84 Ibid., pp. 118f.
85 Ibid., p. 123. Italics in original.
86 Ibid., pp. 123–24.

In summarizing Fetter's theory of interest, Joseph Dorfman wrote:

> Since the impulse to seek immediate gratification was rooted in men's nature, in his theory, the gratification of wants at a future date was not as important as present gratification. Thus he found time value pervading the entire economic structure and the capitalization of psychic income a basic process of human nature. Obviously, he said, these applied more to the relatively permanent goods than to non-durable consumption goods. The capital value of any permanent good, therefore, was the sum of the whole series of rents or incomes it contained, discounted at some rate to its present worth; that is, it was the monetary expression of the psychic incomes yielded by the goods.[87]

In contrast to Böhm-Bawerk's statement of the interest rate problem, Fetter wrote, "It cannot be otherwise in the particular problem of value called capitalization. The first task of scientific study is to state clearly the nature of the problem. In this case it is seen to be the exchange of a present sum of wealth for a series of future rents."[88] In other words, interest arises solely from intertemporal differences in value as expressed in the difference between a present sum of money paid to buy an asset and the future stream of income generated by the asset.

Neoclassical Critics of the PTPT

The interest relationship, Fetter argued, exists in all cases in which a sum of present money is exchanged for a future income stream. Contract loans of all types, production processes of all types, stock shares, and so on all incorporate interest and do so in the same manner. The peculiarities of each case do not affect interest at all. Even in imaginary situations such as those posed by neoclassical economists to dismiss the PTPT, interest persists. Fetter wrote:

---

87 Joseph Dorfman, *The Economic Mind in American Civilization* (New York: Viking Press, 1949), vol. 3, p. 362.
88 Fetter, *Principles of Economics*, p. 125.

> By a flight of scientific imagination we might assume that the stock of indirect agents in the world consisted only of natural food producers, and that this stock and its yield were absolutely unchangeable by man's will or efforts. Each man in such case would have to stand with hands tied, and take the fruits as they matured. Even in such a case there would be capitalization and a rate of discount on future rents. The fruit-tree (that is, the whole future series of fruits) would bear a certain relation to one year's yield; the field would bear a certain relation to its crop. Wherever there are buyers and sellers of more or less durable agents of it matters not what kind or origin, there are present the elements and causes for the fixing of a rate of time discount.[89]

While Fetter anticipated the PTPT response to the challenges to it made by neoclassical economists, Roger Garrison and Israel Kirzner, in their contributions to this volume, recount the PTPT response to cases like Frank Knight's Crusonia plant, Paul Samuelson's rice, and Fisher's sheep, hardtack, and figs. Physical properties of goods and factors do not determine the degree to which people value them or the level of their prices. Value and price are determined by mental judgments people make about the physical properties of goods and factors. A 10 percent annual increase in the physical stock of a Crusonia plant, or a bushel of rice, or a flock of sheep does not dictate any particular time-discount or rate of interest, let alone exactly 10 percent. If the Crusonia plant, or bushel of rice, or flock of sheep were a tradable good in the monetary market and if the time-discount rate was 5 percent, then the rate of interest earned from investing in any one of them would be 5 percent. If, to the contrary, the stream of the discounted marginal revenue product resulted in a capital value for any one of them higher than its purchase price, then investors would bid more heavily to buy it and acquire the resulting net income. Their bidding would push its purchase price up to the level of its capital value and, thereby, reduce the return from owning it to 5 percent. Fisher, Knight,

---

[89] Fetter, *Principles of Economics*, p. 125.

and Samuelson cannot avoid the force of the PTPT logic by constructing conditions in which there can be no trade of the items or, if there is, it cannot be done in money. In such circumstances, as shown above, Fetter demonstrates that the rate of interest cannot emerge at all. By contrast, Böhm-Bawerk's statement of the interest rate problem, "the phenomenon of interest presents, on the whole, a remarkable picture of a lifeless thing, capital, producing an everlasting and inexhaustible supply of goods," does not seem immune to their criticism.[90]

Both Garrison and Kirzner, also, address the claim that the rate of interest is the price of the factor of production called "waiting." As Garrison points out, to make the argument plausible its proponents define "waiting" as supplying present money. If waiting so defined is used within Fetter's framework, it is, at best, superfluous. The rate of interest is the inter-temporal price of money. At the market-clearing rate of interest, the demanders of waiting (present money) value an amount of waiting (present money) they receive more than the larger amount of future money they give up. They have higher pure time preferences. The demanders of waiting (present money) pay interest to acquire waiting (present money) because having it advances them in time toward the attainment of their ends. They prefer the sooner satisfaction of more urgent ends than the later satisfaction of less urgent ends. At the market-clearing rate of interest, suppliers of waiting (present money) value the future money they receive more than the smaller amount of present money they give up. They have lower pure time preferences. The suppliers of waiting (present money) accept interest because they prefer the greater satisfaction gained in the future to the lesser satisfaction given up in the present. Just as in the PTPT, the rate of interest in the waiting theory within Fetter's framework is determined by pure time preference. Therefore, waiting is, at best, a superfluous mediating concept between pure time preference and the rate of interest. If waiting so

---

90 Böhm-Bawerk, *History and Critique*, p. 1.

defined is treated as a factor of production, however, it cannot be integrated into a causal-realist theory. The rental price of a factor of production conforms to its discounted marginal revenue product (DMRP). A factor's MRP is the price of the output it produces multiplied by the amount of output produced by its marginal unit or its marginal physical product (MPP). The MPP is computed by dividing the change in the amount of output by a change in the amount of an input. The MPP of waiting is the interest return earned from investing the present money acquired divided by the sum of present money acquired. For example, if an entrepreneur borrows a million dollars for a year and earns \$50,000 in interest from investing it, the MPP of waiting is equal to \$50,000/year divided by \$1,000,000/year or 0.05. In other words, the MPP of waiting is the rate of interest. Therefore, the argument that the rate of interest is determined by the demand for waiting as a factor of production and its supply commits the fallacy of the vicious circle.

Time Value and Time Discount

Just as Fetter anticipated the PTPT response to neoclassical critics, his analysis of intertemporal differences in value anticipates the PTPT response to recent critics. Fetter recognized two cases of intertemporal differences in value: a present good trading for a future good and present money trading for future money. Time discount, which is the basis for interest operates in both cases, but another factor operates in the case of goods, namely, the timing of the use of the good. The sum of the two operating factors is time value. Fetter wrote:

> Time value is the difference between the values of things at different times.... The simplest and clearest case of time-value is the difference noticeable in the same thing at different moments. Is this good worth more now or next week? Shall this apple be eaten now or next winter? These questions can be answered only after comparing the marginal utilities

which differ according to the varying conditions of the two periods.

All the other cases of time-value can, by the practical device of substituting the other goods of equivalent value, be reduced to the typical case of comparison of the same thing at different times.[91]

In the first case, different circumstances can arise at different moments in time for using a good as a means and therefore, the value of the end satisfied by the means can differ at different moments in time. A person would select to use the means at that moment in time that generates the greatest value, which depends on the circumstances of using the good at that moment. Since the circumstances for using a good could be more favorable, less favorable, or equally favorable at different moments in time, if a good is traded intertemporally, its forward price could be greater than, less than, or equal to its spot price.

In the second case, the value to be acquired at any moment in time is the same. Timing makes no difference. In this case, intertemporal exchange always places a premium on the present over the future. As Fetter recognized, separating the two factors of time value so that the "equivalent value" aspect can be isolated requires monetary exchange. He wrote:

> But two or more quite different things may be expressed in terms of another thing and so be made comparable. Money becomes the value-unit through which different things may be reduced to the same terms for comparison. With this mode of expressing the value-equivalence of various goods, the interest contract first becomes possible, money (the standard of deferred payments) being the thing exchanged (possibly only in name) at two periods of time. What is really being compared are various gratifications which may be produced by very different material things or services. In its last analysis comparison of values at different points in time must be a comparison of psychic incomes, of two sums of gratification.

---

[91] Fetter, *Principles of Economics*, p. 141.

The comparison of the value of a bushel of apples with that of a barrel of potatoes or a suit of clothes at the same moment appears simple enough. When all are expressed in terms of money, the comparison of each with its value-equivalent at a later date becomes easy.[92]

Fetter recognized that money makes what Mises called economic calculation possible and extended Mises's claim, that money makes the appraisements of all the different goods and factors of production commensurable, from present exchanges to intertemporal exchange. On money as the common unit of value, Fetter wrote:

> Money serves as a "common denominator," for, as all other things can be expressed in terms of money, through it the value of other things can be compared. The other things can be expressed in money because they are constantly exchanged for it. All things being compared with money, can in turn be compared with each other.[93]

The advantage of money in economic calculation made it "almost inevitable, that the common denominator in which all values are expressed from day to day should continue to be taken as the value unit when the completion of the exchange is delayed a day, a month, or a year," wrote Fetter.[94] The emergence of the rate of interest from the intertemporal exchange of money, completes the system of economic calculation. He wrote:

> The market rate of interest thus extends over all forms of wealth and pervades every phase of business. The value of every durable agent is fixed with reference to a prevailing interest rate, through the discounting to their worth of all the incomes it is believed to contain.[95]

In summarizing the importance of money as a common denominator, Fetter wrote:

---

92 Fetter, *Principles of Economics*, pp. 141–42.
93 Ibid., p. 104.
94 Ibid., p. 105.
95 Ibid., p. 149.

It is this expression of the value of all other things in terms of money which may well be deemed the essential characteristic of the capitalistic age. In earlier periods wealth was thought of and expressed in concrete terms; now it is expressed in money. The general use of money affects men's ways of looking at wealth and speaking of it. Without appreciating the nature and function of money, it is impossible to grasp the significance of capital in modern industry.[96]

While money makes the isolation of the time discount factor possible, its use in intertemporal exchange obscured the underlying causes of interest which led to numerous fallacies. "The simplicity and obviousness of time-value in the case of money loans at interest led men at first to recognize that phase of the problem exclusively," Fetter wrote, "and later the term 'interest,' not without much confusion of thought, was given a wider significance."[97]

The wider significance comes from the fact that, "time-value," Fetter wrote, "is here understood to be that all-pervading difference in the values of uses and gratifications of wealth at different points of time."[98] "Indeed time difference in value is a universal phenomenon of life and conduct," he wrote, one that is "more varied and pervasive ... than has usually been recognized in popular or economic discussion of the subject of interest."[99]

Fetter did not use the term "time preference" in *Principles of Economics*. With the publication of *Economic Principles*, eleven years later, he made time preference the first concept he discusses under the section "Time-Value and Interest." Time preference refers to the overall preference a person has for present goods relative to future goods as expressed in his intertemporal choice. Thus, time preference, like time-value could in some cases favor the present and some cases favor the future.[100] In referring to the

---

96 Fetter, *Principles of Economics*, p. 107.
97 Ibid., p. 142.
98 Ibid., p. 151.
99 Ibid., pp. 144–45.
100 Fetter, *Economic Principles*, pp. 235–39.

aspect of time-value he called time discount, i.e., "that present goods are always worth more than future goods of like kind and quality," Fetter uses the term "pure time preference."[101] In cases that mix the two time aspects together, "there is no element of *pure* time preference," Fetter wrote, "no degree of preference for the present unit simply because it *is* present."[102]

Pure time preference exists in every intertemporal choice and, therefore, so does interest. Fetter wrote:

> Before ever a money-loan was made, before even money had come into existence in the world, time-preference existed. It lies in the very nature of choice by animals and by savages. In many ways it is interwoven into the valuations of every self-sufficing economy in the days of barter. It becomes generalized as a prevailing rate in each individual's economy and as a price for timeliness in all exchanges of goods and uses of different time-periods. The rate becomes equalized as between different series of uses, as the rate of time preference and of time-price cannot consistently be greatly unequal within any circle where time-choice is possible. The use of money in trade gave much greater exactness to this time-price as embodied in goods and to their prices in relation to the times of their use. Today in the innumerable valuations of many business enterprises where there is no monetary borrowing or lending time-preference expresses itself in the capitalization (price) of the durative agents of the environment. Every loan of money (or of goods in terms of money) at interest therefore occurs where the price of goods already embodies this premium on the present possession.[103]

Not only the rate of interest, but the balance between saving and consumption is determined by pure time preference. Fetter wrote:

> Evidently somewhere between these two extremes [i.e., preference for the future that endangers a person's life for lack of

---

101 Fetter, *Economic Principles*, p. 239.
102 Ibid., p. 249. Italics in original.
103 Ibid., pp. 310–11.

present goods and preference for the present that condemns a person to hand-to-mouth subsistence] there must be, in each economy, a ratio of exchange between present and future, which in fact is the interest rate. This rate applied to utilities traces through each good a line analogous to the isothermal line on the map, marking off a zone of utilities for the present and other zones for each period of the future. There is thus a close relation between saving and the rate of time-discount.[104]

In the market, capitalization of the stream of MRP from using a durable producer good will result in its price. Entrepreneurs use these asset prices to allocate durable producer goods into the higher-valued production processes and resources into the higher-valued lines of investment. While prices vary widely from one asset to another, the interest rate that discounts the MRP stream of durable producer goods will be uniform across all production processes of the same time structure.

As the excerpt from *Human Action*, included in this volume, shows Ludwig von Mises accepted Fetter's PTPT of interest, although he failed to give Fetter proper credit in developing the theory. In Mises's view, "economics owes the time-preference theory to William Stanley Jevons and its elaboration, most of all, to Eugen von Böhm-Bawerk."[105] Fetter's contribution was in helping to perfect the theory. "It was on the foundation laid by him [i.e., Böhm-Bawerk]," Mises wrote, "that later economists—foremost among them Knut Wicksell, Frank Albert Fetter and Irving Fisher—were successful in perfecting the time-preference theory."[106] Rothbard also downplayed Fetter, but on the grounds of his broad definition of time preference. "Whereas Fetter believed that people could have either positive or negative rates of time preference," Rothbard wrote, "Mises demonstrated that a positive rate is deducible from the fact of human action."[107]

---

104 Fetter, *Principles of Economics*, p. 160.
105 Ludwig von Mises, *Human Action: A Treatise on Economics*, scholar's edition (Auburn, Ala.: Ludwig von Mises Institute, 1998), p. 485.
106 Ibid., p. 486.
107 Murray N. Rothbard, "Time Preference," reprinted in this volume, p. 66.

But this is merely a terminological, not conceptual, distinction. As discussed above, Fetter used the phrase pure time preference, which was based on time-discount, for what Mises referred to as time preference and he used the phrase time preference to refer to choice based on time value, which incorporates both time-discount and the timing of an action. Mises defined time preference in the narrow sense of the time-discount of a satisfaction later compared to the same satisfaction sooner. Mises wrote, "satisfaction of a want in the nearer future is, other things being equal, preferred to that in the farther distant future."[108] While their semantics differ, the conceptual framework of Mises and Fetter is the same.[109]

Mises refined and improved the pure time preference theory, especially in supplanting Fetter's more psychological conception of value with a praxeological conception, but by dropping Fetter's more inclusive set of concepts he opened the theory to objections that can be dealt with more easily in Fetter's system. As Garrison makes clear, neoclassical economists came to define time preference "in terms of the time pattern of consumption preferred by the individual."[110] Time preference would be positive, neutral, or negative depending on whether a person choose a consumption pattern skewed toward the present, uniform across time, or skewed toward the future. As we have seen, Fetter's concept of time preference incorporates both the consideration of the MU of units of a good consumed in different time periods and the time-discount. The latter determines the rate of interest apart from the former. Time-discount also influences temporal allocation by setting the discount of the future and the extent of saving relative to consumption, but does not dictate a particular temporal

---

108 Mises, *Human Action*, pp. 480–81.
109 Perhaps, Mises and Rothbard underappreciated Fetter because they relied more heavily on Fetter's later work, *Economic Principles*, to understand Fetter's views instead of his earlier work, *Principles of Economics*, in which he carefully sets out his conceptual framework.
110 Roger Garrison, "In Defense of the Misesian Theory of Interests," reprinted in this volume, p. 87.

pattern of consumption, which is determined instead by time value. In Fetter's view, it is not possible for the time-discount to emerge unalloyed with the other component of time-value in the intertemporal exchange of goods. An apple consumed in a week may have a higher MU than an apple consumed today because of the different conditions of consumption in a week compared to today. If this MU next week is high enough, even when the time-discount is applied, a person may favor an apple in a week to an apple today and therefore, exchange a present apple for a future apple at a premium for the future instead of the present. Unlike all other goods, the timing of holding a unit of money does not affect its usefulness as a means to the end to which it is put, i.e., as a medium of exchange. Fetter wrote:

> In every case where money is retained for a time in possession, there is expected from it a usufruct as great as, or greater than, can be secured from anything else for which it can be exchanged. This usufruct is a net surplus, or income, yielded by a sum of money undiminished in amount up to the moment it is spent.... Because money yields a rent men make the sacrifice involved in keeping a stock of it on hand. On this rent is based that part of the value of money that is derived from its money use. As the use of money as a standard of deferred payment, or basis of commercial obligations, does not require that it be owned by the parties writing the contract, this use of money is a free good, a sort of social by-product of the medium of exchange.[III]

Because the moment in time that a unit of money is held does not affect its usefulness, money serves as a common denominator in intertemporal, as well as present, exchanges. The exchange of present money for future money, therefore, isolates the time-discount or pure time preference factor and permits the emergence of a pure rate of interest.

Failure to adopt Fetter's conceptual framework led Mises to conflate two different comparisons of value under his definition of time preference. He wrote that time preference referred to

---

III Fetter, *Principles of Economics*, pp. 106–07.

comparing a satisfaction earlier with the same satisfaction later and "present goods are more valuable than future goods."[112] To avoid the problem of cases in which a good in the future is valued more highly than the same good in the present, Mises asserts that a good in a different temporal position, just as a good in a different geographic position, is really a different good. In analyzing the case of a person in wintertime preferring ice in the summer to ice in winter, Mises concludes, "The two things are for all practical purposes different commodities."[113] Although this assertion preserves his claim that a higher future than present price for a good does not contradict the time preference theory of interest, it is inconsistent with his claim that time preference ensures that "present goods are more valuable than future goods" and it fails to explain how the rate of interest can emerge in intertemporal markets.

Contrast that with Fetter's analysis of the same case. He wrote:

> Ice may be stored in midwinter when it is all but a free good and a little labor serves to fill the ice-house. Kept until the summer months, the ice rises in value as the desire for it grows. Likewise the higher price secured by the owner of a thing kept for sale to others, reflects the change in utility, and affords practically a rent which is the motive for investing capital in that business. Any saver or abstainer puts aside present wants only when the future good, with the addition of time-value of money interest, appears as large as the present good. Interest is therefore the equalizer of the value of things in different periods. Put into the scale of judgment when present and future are compared, it helps to balance the disparity in the gratifications given by economic goods in different periods of time.[114]

Fetter faces no need to reconcile the fact of the higher future price of ice with the rate of interest by deeming ice in the

---

[112] Mises, *Human Action*, p. 481.
[113] Ibid., pp. 486–87.
[114] Fetter, *Principles of Economics*, p. 162.

summer a different good from ice in the winter. Neither the intertemporal exchange of ice nor of any other good, save money, isolates pure time preference and therefore, ensures a premium of the present.

Recent Critics of the PTPT

It is precisely issues of this type with the PTPT as presented by Mises and Rothbard that concern recent critics of the PTPT. Robert Murphy offers two related criticisms of the PTPT.[115] First, he poses a dilemma for the PTPT. If time preference is defined as the preference for a given satisfaction sooner over the same satisfaction later, then it ensures a premium of the present, but has no logical connection to the exchange of present goods against future goods, which can trade at a premium for the present or a premium of the future. If time preference is defined as the preference for present goods over future goods, then it has a logical connection with the exchange of present goods against future goods but cannot ensure the existence of a positive rate of interest.[116] But the horns of this dilemma are evaded by recognizing Fetter's distinction about the underlying sources of intertemporal exchange ratios. The exchange of present money for future money isolates pure time preference and permits the emergence of the rate of interest as the intertemporal exchange ratio of present money for future money. The exchange ratio between a present good and a future good is not the rate of interest, but is based on time value, and could either have a premium of the present or a premium of the future. Second, Murphy argues that if pure time preference theorists define time preference in terms of satisfactions and not goods, then time preference is neither necessary nor sufficient to explain the rate of interest as defined as the intertemporal exchange rate of goods.[117] This criticism also

---

115 Robert P. Murphy, *Unanticipated Intertemporal Exchange in Theories of Interest*, Doctoral Dissertation (New York: New York University, 2003).
116 Ibid., pp. 65–76.
117 Ibid., pp. 76–91.

misses the mark since in the PTPT the rate of interest is not the intertemporal exchange rate of goods. With the intertemporal exchange of money, pure time preference is both necessary and sufficient to explain the pure rate of interest.

Fetter's distinction between time value and pure time preference also applies to Guido Hülsmann's argument that Mises's time preference theory fails because it makes two contradictory claims.[118] First, Mises claims that a larger stock of a future good is somehow inherently more valuable than a smaller stock of the good in the present and therefore, the only reason a person chooses the present is time preference. Second, Mises claims that something in the present is a different good from the same thing in the future. If the second claim is true, then a larger amount of a good in the future compared to the present does not imply a greater value of the larger amount of the good in the future over the smaller amount in the present. But, as seen above, the PTPT need make neither claim. In Fetter's framework, pure time preference exists whether a person chooses present goods over future goods or vice versa. The evidence of pure time preference lies elsewhere. And Fetter does not assert that something in the future is a different good from the same thing in the present in order to preserve the PTPT. His view is that the different value of something in the future compared to its value in the present depends on the different circumstances in the two time periods. Interest has nothing to do with this aspect of time value, but stems instead from the difference between a given satisfaction when attained sooner instead of later. Since this is also Mises's view, his time preference theory is immune from this criticism. His view only appears to be susceptible to this criticism because he failed to adopt Fetter's more robust framework.

Hülsmann also asserts that Mises's conception of time preference differs from that of his predecessors like Böhm-Bawerk and Fetter. They thought of time preference as the difference

---

[118] Jörg Guido Hülsmann, "A Theory of Interest," *Quarterly Journal of Austrian Economics* 5, no. 4 (Winter 2002): 81.

between the value of present goods and future goods, whereas Mises thought of it as the difference between the options of choice in a single action, i.e., the difference between the use of some good sooner and the same good later.[119] But, as seen above, Fetter also saw pure time preference as being isolated in the exchange of a present good, money, for the same good in the future. Hülsmann's claim that for Mises, "time preference thus concerns the value differential between that use of the good that comes to be realized in the present, and an alternative future use of this good that could have been realized if a different choice had been made," is true for money in Fetter's view as well.[120] Hülsmann claims, correctly, that in making a comparison of the present value of a good with its future value would involve the value of the timing of using the good. But, as we have seen, this is not true for money. It is only Mises's description of the PTPT that is subject to Hülsmann's criticism that "time preference, in the sense Mises understood the term, concerns the timing of achieving one's ends."[121] Fetter's exposition of the PTPT is not subject to this criticism. Moreover, money prices make the monetary sum for any collection of goods commensurable with the monetary sum for any other collection of goods. A present sum of money for any collection of goods can be made commensurable with a future sum of money for any other collection of goods as well. A person can, at the present moment, compare the value of a present sum of money as a medium of exchange with the anticipated value of the same sum of money as a medium of exchange in the future. Such a comparison isolates the pure time preference factor in time value. When people exchange present money for future money based on such comparisons at any moment, the pure rate of interest results.

Resolving the debate between recent critics and defenders of the PTPT, however, is a chapter in the history of interest rate

---

[119] Hülsmann, "Theory of Interest," 83–84.
[120] Ibid., 83.
[121] Ibid., 85.

theories yet to be written. It would be unwise to count out the PTPT. As Kirzner writes, "for almost a century a particular theory of interest has been again and again discussed, refuted, defended, ignored, forgotten, and rediscovered; somehow it has managed to survive."[122]

Jeffrey M. Herbener
Grove City, Pennsylvania
June 2011

---

[122] Israel Kirzner, "The Pure Time-Preference Theory of Interest: An Attempt at Clarification"; reprinted in this volume, p. 99.

Time Preference

{ *By Murray N. Rothbard* }

Time Preference is the insight that people prefer "present goods" (goods available for use at present) to "future goods" (present expectations of goods becoming available at some date in the future), and that the social rate of time preference, the result of the interactions of individual time-preference schedules, will determine and be equal to the pure rate of interest in a society. The economy is pervaded by a time market for present as against future goods, not only in the market for loans (in which creditors trade present money for the right to receive money in the future), but also as a "natural rate" in all processes of production. For capitalists pay out present money to buy or rent land, capital goods, and raw materials, and to hire labor (as well as buying labor outright in a system of slavery), thereby purchasing expectations of future revenue from the eventual sales of product. Long-run profit rates and rates of return on capital are therefore forms of interest rate. As businessmen seek to gain

---

First published in *The New Palgrave: A Dictionary of Economics*, John Eatwell, Murray Milgate, and Peter Newman, eds., 4 vols. (London and New York: Macmillan, 1990 [1987]) and reprinted in *The New Palgrave Dictionary*, 2nd ed., Steven N. Durlauf and Lawrence E. Blume, eds. (New York: Palgrave Macmillan, 2008).

profits and avoid losses, the economy will tend toward a general equilibrium, in which all interest rates and rates of return will be equal, and hence there will be no pure entrepreneurial profits or losses.

In centuries of wrestling with the vexed question of the justification of interest, the Catholic scholastic philosophers arrived at highly sophisticated explanations and justifications of return on capital, including risk and the opportunity cost of profit forgone. But they had extreme difficulty with the interest on a riskless loan, and hence denounced all such interest as sinful and usurious.

Some of the later scholastics, however, in their more favorable view of usury, began to approach a time preference explanation of interest. During a comprehensive demolition of the standard arguments for the prohibition of usury in his *Treatise on Contracts* (1499), Conrad Summenhart (1465–1511), theologian at the University of Tübingen, used time preference to justify the purchase of a discounted debt, even if the debt be newly created. When someone pays $100 for the right to obtain $110 at a future date, the buyer (lender) doesn't profit usuriously from the loan because both he and the seller (borrower) value the future $110 as being worth $100 at the present time.[1]

A half-century later, the distinguished Dominican canon lawyer and monetary theorist at the University of Salamanca, Martín de Azpilcueta Navarrus (1493–1586) clearly set forth the concept of time preference, but failed to apply it to a defense of usury. In his *Commentary on Usury* (1556), Azpilcueta pointed out that a present good, such as money, will naturally be worth more on the market than future goods, that is, claims to money in the future. As Azpilcueta put it:

> a claim on something is worth less than the thing itself, and … it is plain that that which is not usable for a year is less

---

[1] J.T. Noonan, Jr., *The Scholastic Analysis of Usury* (Cambridge, Mass.: Harvard University Press, 1957).

valuable than something of the same quality which is usable at once.²

At about the same time, the Italian humanist and politician Gian Francesco Lottini da Volterra, in his handbook of advice to princes, *Avvedimenti civili* (1574), discovered time preference. Unfortunately, Lottini also inaugurated the tradition of moralistically deploring time preference as an overestimation of a present that can be grasped immediately by the senses.³

Two centuries later, the Neapolitan abbé, Ferdinando Galiani (1728–1887), revived the rudiments of time-preference in his *Della Moneta* (1751).⁴ Galiani pointed out that just as the exchange rate of two currencies equates the value of a present and a spatially distant money, so the rate of interest equates present with future, or temporally distant, money. What is being equated is not physical properties, but subjective values in the minds of individuals.

These scattered hints scarcely prepare one for the remarkable development of a full-scale time-preference theory of interest by the French statesman, Anne Robert Jacques Turgot (1727–1781), who, in a relatively few hastily written contributions, anticipated almost completely the later Austrian theory of capital and interest.⁵ In the course of a paper defending usury, Turgot asked: why are borrowers willing to pay an interest premium for the use of money? The focus should not be on the amount of metal repaid but on the usefulness of the money to the lender and borrower. In particular, Turgot compares the "difference in usefulness which exists at the date of borrowing between a sum currently owned and an equal sum which is to be received at

---

2 Barry Gordon, *Economic Analysis before Adam Smith: Hesiod to Lessius* (New York: Barnes & Noble, 1975), p. 215.
3 Emil Kauder, *A History of Marginal Utility Theory* (Princeton, N.J.: Princeton University Press, 1965), pp. 19–22.
4 Arthur E. Monroe, ed., *Early Economic Thought* (Cambridge, Mass.: Harvard University Press, 1924).
5 A.J.R. Turgot, *The Economics of A.J.R. Turgot*, Peter D. Groenewegen, ed. (The Hague: Martinus Nijhoff, 1977).

a distant date," and notes the well-known motto, "a bird in the hand is better than two in the bush." Since the sum of money owned now "is preferable to the assurance of receiving a similar sum in one or several years' time," returning the same principal means that the lender "gives the money and receives only an assurance." Therefore, interest compensates for this difference in value by a sum proportionate to the length of the delay. Turgot added that what must be compared in a loan transaction is not the value of money lent with the value repaid, but rather the "value of the *promise* of a sum of money compared to the value of money available now."[6]

In addition, Turgot was apparently the first to arrive at the concept of *capitalization*, a corollary to time preference, which holds that the present capital value of any durable good will tend to equal the sum of its expected annual rents, or returns, discounted by the market rate of time preference, or rate of interest.

Turgot also pioneered in analyzing the relation between the quantity of money and interest rates. If an increased supply of money goes to low time-preference people, then the increased proportion of savings to consumption lowers time preferences and hence interest rates fall while prices rise. But if an increased quantity goes into the hands of high time-preference people, the opposite would happen and interest rates would rise along with prices. Generally, over recent centuries, he noted, the spirit of thrift has been growing in Europe and hence time-preference rates and interest rates have tended to fall.

One of the notable injustices in the historiography of economic thought was Böhm-Bawerk's brusque dismissal in 1884 of Turgot's anticipation of his own time-preference theory of interest as merely a "land fructification theory."[7] Partly this dismissal stemmed from Böhm's methodology of clearing the ground for his own positive theory of interest by demolishing, and hence

---

6 Turgot, *The Economics of A.R.J. Turgot*, pp. 158–59.
7 Eugen von Böhm-Bawerk, *Capital and Interest*, 4th ed. (South Holland, Ill.: Libertarian Press, 1959 [1884]), vol. I.

sometimes doing injustice to, his own forerunners.⁸ The unfairness is particularly glaring in the case of Turgot, because we now know that in 1876, only eight years before the publication of his history of theories of interest, Böhm-Bawerk wrote a glowing tribute to Turgot's theory of interest in an as yet unpublished paper in Karl Knies's seminar at the University of Heidelberg.⁹

In the course of his demolition of the Ricardo–James Mill labor theory of value on behalf of a subjective utility theory, Samuel Bailey clearly set forth the concept of time preference. Rebutting Mill's statement that time, as a "mere abstract word," could not add to value, Bailey declared that "we generally prefer a present pleasure or enjoyment to a distant one," and therefore prefer present goods to waiting for goods to arrive in the future. Bailey, however, did not go on to apply his insight to interest.¹⁰

In the mid-1830s, the Irish economist Samuel Mountifort Longfield worked out the later Austrian theory of capital as performing the service for workers of supplying money at present instead of waiting for the future when the product will be sold. In turn the capitalist receives from the workers a time discount from their productivity. As Longfield put it, the capitalist

> pays the wages immediately, and in return receives the value of [the worker's] labour, ... [which] is greater than the wages of that labour. The difference is the profit made by the capitalist for his advances ... as it were, the discount which the labourer pays for prompt payment.¹¹

The "pre-Austrian" time analysis of capital and interest was most fully worked out, in the same year, 1834, by the Scottish

---

8 Knut Wicksell, "Böhm-Bawerk's Theory of Interest," in Knut Wicksell, *Selected Papers on Economic Theory*, E. Lindahl, ed. (Cambridge, Mass.: Harvard University Press, 1958 [1911]), p. 177.
9 Turgot, *The Economics of A.R.J. Turgot*, pp. xxix–xxx.
10 Samuel Bailey, *A Critical Dissertation on the Nature, Measure, and Causes of Value* (New York: Augustus M. Kelley, 1967 [1825]).
11 S.M. Longfield, *The Economic Writings of Mountifort Longfield*, R.D.C. Black, ed. (Clifton, N.J.: Augustus M. Kelley, 1971).

and Canadian eccentric John Rae (1786–1872). In the course of attempting an anti-Smithian defense of the protective tariff, Rae, in his *Some New Principles on the Subject of Political Economy* (1834), developed the Böhm-Bawerkian time analysis of capital, pointing out that investment lengthens the time involved in the processes of production. Rae noted that the capitalist must weigh the greater productivity of longer production processes against waiting for them to come to fruition. Capitalists will sacrifice present money for a greater return in the future, the difference—the interest return—reflecting the social rate of time preference. Rae saw that people's time preference rates reflect their cultural and psychological willingness to take a shorter or longer view of the future. His moral preferences were clearly with the low time-preference thrifty as against the high time-preference people who suffer from a "defect of the imagination." Rae's analysis had little impact on economics until resurrected at the turn of the twentieth century, whereupon it was generously hailed in the later editions of Böhm-Bawerk's history of interest theories.[12]

Time preference, as a concept and as a foundation for the explanation of interest, has been an outstanding feature of the Austrian School of economics. Its founder, Carl Menger (1840–1921), enunciated the concept of time preference in 1871, pointing out that satisfying the immediate needs of life and health are necessarily prerequisites for satisfying more remote future needs. In addition, Menger declared, "all experience teaches that we humans consider a present pleasure, or one expected in the near future, more important than one of the same intensity which is not expected to occur until some more distant times."[13] But Menger never extended time preference from his value theory to a theory of interest; and when his follower Böhm-Bawerk did

---

12   Böhm-Bawerk, *Capital and Interest*, vol. 1.
13   Knut Wicksell, "The New Edition of Menger's *Grundsätze*," in Wicksell, *Selected Papers on Economic Theory*, p. 195. And Carl Menger, *Principles of Economics*, James Dingwall and Bert Hoselitz, eds. (Glencoe, Ill.: Free Press, 1950 [1871]), pp. 153–54.

so, he peevishly deleted this discussion from the second edition of his *Principles of Economics*.[14]

Böhm-Bawerk's *Capital and Interest* (1884) is the *locus classicus* of the time–preference theory of interest. In his first, historical volume, he demolished all other theories, in particular the productivity theory of interest; but five years later, in his *Positive Theory of Capital* (1889), Böhm-Bawerk brought back the productivity theory in an attempt to combine it with a time-preference explanation of interest.[15] In his "three grounds" for the explanation of interest, time preference constituted two, and the greater productivity of longer processes of production the third, Böhm-Bawerk ironically placing greatest importance upon the third ground. Influenced strongly by Böhm-Bawerk, Irving Fisher increasingly took the same path of stressing the marginal productivity of capital as the main determinant of interest.[16]

With the work of Böhm-Bawerk and Fisher, the modern theory of interest was set squarely on the path of placing time preference in a subordinate role in the explanation of interest, determining only the rate of consumer loans and the supply of consumer savings, while the alleged productivity of capital determines the more important demand for loans and for savings. Hence, modern interest theory fails to integrate interest on consumer loans and producers' returns into a coherent explanation.

In contrast, Frank A. Fetter, building on Böhm-Bawerk, completely discarded productivity as an explanation of interest and constructed an integrated theory of value and distribution in which interest is determined solely by time preference, while marginal productivity determines the "rental prices" of the factors of production.[17] In his outstanding critique of Böhm-Bawerk,

---

14 Wicksell, "New Edition of Menger's *Grundsätze*," pp. 195–56.
15 Böhm-Bawerk, *Capital and Interest*, vols. 1 and 2.
16 Irving Fisher, *The Rate of Interest* (New York: Macmillan, 1907) and *The Theory of Interest* (New York: Kelley and Millman, 1954 [1930]).
17 Frank A. Fetter, *Economic Principles* (New York: The Century Co., 1915), vol. 1 and Frank A. Fetter, *Capital, Interest, and Rent: Essays in the Theory of Distribution*, Murray N. Rothbard, ed. (Kansas City: Sheed Andrews and McMeel, 1977).

Fetter pointed out a fundamental error of the third ground in trying to explain the return on capital as "present goods" earning a return for their productivity in the future; instead, capital goods are *future* goods, since they are only valuable in the expectation of being used to produce goods that will be sold to the consumer at a future date.[18] One way of seeing the fallacy of a productivity explanation of interest is to look at the typical practice of any current microeconomics text: after explaining marginal productivity as determining the demand curve for factors with wage rates on the y-axis, the textbook airily shifts to interest rates on the y-axis to illustrate the marginal productivity determination of interest. But the analog on the y-axis should not be interest, which is a ratio and not a price, but rather the *rental price* (price per unit time) of a capital good. Thus, interest remains totally unexplained. In short, as Fetter pointed out, marginal productivity determines rental prices, and time preference determines the rate of interest, while the capital value of a factor of production is the expected sum of future rents from a durable factor discounted by the rate of time preference or interest.

The leading economist adopting Fetter's pure time preference view of interest was Ludwig von Mises, in his *Human Action*.[19] Mises amended the theory in two important ways. First, he rid the concept of its moralistic tone, which had been continued by Böhm-Bawerk, implicitly criticizing people for "under"-estimating the future. Mises made clear that a positive time preference rate is an essential attribute of human nature. Second, and as a corollary, whereas Fetter believed that people could have either positive or negative rates of time preference, Mises demonstrated that a positive rate is deducible from the fact of human action, since by the very nature of a goal or an end people wish to achieve that goal as soon as possible.

---

18 Frank A. Fetter, "The 'Roundabout Process' in the Interest Theory," *Quarterly Journal of Economics* 17 (November, 1902): 163–80. Reprinted in Fetter, *Capital, Interest, and Rent*.

19 Ludwig von Mises, *Human Action: A Treatise on Economics*, 3rd rev. ed. (Chicago: Regnery, 1966).

Human Action: The Rate of Interest

{ *By Ludwig von Mises* }

The Phenomenon of Interest

It has been shown that time preference is a category inherent in every human action. Time preference manifests itself in the phenomenon of originary interest, i.e., the discount of future goods as against present goods.

Interest is not merely interest on capital. Interest is not the specific income derived from the utilization of capital goods. The correspondence between three factors of production—labor, capital, and land—and three classes of income—wages, profit, and rent—as taught by the classical economists is untenable. Rent is not the specific revenue from land. Rent is a general catallactic phenomenon; it plays in the yield of labor and capital goods the same role it plays in the yield of land. Furthermore there is no homogeneous source of income that could be called profit in the sense in which the classical economists applied this term. Profit (in the sense of entrepreneurial profit) and interest are no more characteristic of capital than they are of land.

Reprinted from *Human Action: A Treatise on Economics*, Scholar's edition (Auburn, Ala.: Ludwig von Mises Institute, 2008).

The prices of consumers' goods are by the interplay of the forces operating on the market apportioned to the various complementary factors cooperating in their production. As the consumers' goods are present goods, while the factors of production are means for the production of future goods, and as present goods are valued higher than future goods of the same kind and quantity, the sum thus apportioned, even in the imaginary construction of the evenly rotating economy, falls behind the present price of the consumers' goods concerned. This difference is the originary interest. It is not specifically connected with any of the three classes of factors of production which the classical economists distinguished. Entrepreneurial profit and loss are produced by changes in the data and the resulting price changes which occur in the passing of the period of production.

Naïve reasoning does not see any problem in the current revenue derived from hunting, fishing, cattle breeding, forestry, and agriculture. Nature generates deer, fish, and cattle and makes them grow, causes the cows to give milk and the chickens to lay eggs, the trees to put on wood and to bear fruit, and the seeds to shoot into ears. He who has a title to appropriate for himself this recurring wealth enjoys a steady income. Like a stream which continually carries new water, the "stream of income" flows continually and conveys again and again new wealth. The whole process is plainly a natural phenomenon. But for the economist a problem is presented in the determination of prices for land, cattle, and all the rest. If future goods were not bought and sold at a discount as against present goods, the buyer of land would have to pay a price which equals the sum of all future net revenues and which would leave nothing for a current reiterated income.

The yearly recurring proceeds of the owners of land and cattle are not marked by any characteristic which would catallactically distinguish them from the proceeds stemming from produced factors of production which are used up sooner or later in the processes of production. The power of disposal over a piece of land is the control of this field's cooperation in the production of all the fruit which can ever be grown on it, and the power of disposal over a mine is the control of its cooperation in the extraction of all the minerals which can ever be brought to the surface from it. In the same way the ownership of a machine or a bale of cotton is the control of its cooperation in the manufacture of all goods which are produced with its cooperation. The fundamental fallacy implied in all the productivity and use approaches to the problem of interest was that they traced back the phenomenon of interest to these productive services rendered by the factors of production. However, the serviceableness of the factors of production determines the prices paid for them, not interest. These prices exhaust the whole difference between the productivity of a process aided by a definite factor's cooperation and that of a process lacking this cooperation. The difference between the sum of the prices of the complementary factors of production and the products which emerges even in the absence of changes in the market data concerned, is an outcome of the higher valuation of present goods as compared with future goods. As production goes on, the factors of production are transformed or ripen into present goods of a higher value. This increment is the source of specific proceeds flowing into the hands of the owners of the factors of production, of originary interest.

The owners of the material factors of production—as distinct from the pure entrepreneurs of the imaginary construction of an integration of catallactic functions—harvest two catallactically different items: the prices paid for the productive cooperation of the factors they control on the one hand and interest on the other hand. These two things must not be confused. It is not permissible to refer, in the explanation of interest, to the services rendered by the factors of production in the turning out of products.

Interest is a homogeneous phenomenon. There are no different sources of interest. Interest on durable goods and interest on consumption-credit are like other kinds of interest an outgrowth of the higher valuation of present goods as against future goods.

Originary Interest

Originary interest is the ratio of the value assigned to want-satisfaction in the immediate future and the value assigned to want-satisfaction in remoter periods of the future. It manifests itself in the market economy in the discount of future goods as against present goods. It is a ratio of commodity prices, not a price in itself. There prevails a tendency toward the equalization of this ratio for all commodities. In the imaginary construction of the evenly rotating economy the rate of originary interest is the same for all commodities.

Originary interest is not "the price paid for the services of capital."[1] The higher productivity of more time-consuming roundabout methods of production which is referred to by Böhm-Bawerk and by some later economists in the explanation of interest, does not explain the phenomenon. It is, on the contrary, the phenomenon of originary interest that explains why less time-consuming methods of production are resorted to in spite of the fact that more time-consuming methods would render a higher output per unit of input. Moreover, the phenomenon of originary interest explains why pieces of usable land can be sold and bought at finite prices. If the future services which a piece of land can render were to be valued in the same way in which its present services are valued, no finite price would be high enough to impel its owner to sell it. Land could neither be bought nor sold against definite amounts of money, nor bartered against goods which can render only a finite number of services. Pieces of land would be bartered only against other pieces of land. A superstructure that can yield during a period of ten years an annual revenue of one hundred dollars would be priced (apart from the soil on which it is built) at the beginning of this period at one thousand dollars, at the beginning of the second year at nine hundred dollars, and so on.

---

1 This is the popular definition of interest as, for instance, given by Richard T. Ely, Thomas S. Adams, Max O. Lorenz, and Allyn A. Young, *Outlines of Economics*, 3rd ed. (New York: Macmillan, 1920), p. 493.

Originary interest is not a price determined on the market by the interplay of the demand for and the supply of capital or capital goods. Its height does not depend on the extent of this demand and supply. It is rather the rate of originary interest that determines both the demand for and the supply of capital and capital goods. It determines how much of the available supply of goods is to be devoted to consumption in the immediate future and how much to provision for remoter periods of the future.

People do not save and accumulate capital because there is interest. Interest is neither the impetus to saving nor the reward or the compensation granted for abstaining from immediate consumption. It is the ratio in the mutual valuation of present goods as against future goods.

The loan market does not determine the rate of interest. It adjusts the rate of interest on loans to the rate of originary interest as manifested in the discount of future goods.

Originary interest is a category of human action. It is operative in any valuation of external things and can never disappear. If one day the state of affairs were to return which was actual at the close of the first millennium of the Christian era when people believed that the ultimate end of all earthly things was impending, men would stop providing for future secular wants. The factors of production would in their eyes become useless and worthless. The discount of future goods as against present goods would not vanish. It would, on the contrary, increase beyond all measure. On the other hand, the fading away of originary interest would mean that people do not care at all for want-satisfaction in nearer periods of the future. It would mean that they prefer to an apple available today, tomorrow, in one year or in ten years, two apples available in a thousand or ten thousand years.

We cannot even think of a world in which originary interest would not exist as an inexorable element in every kind of action. Whether there is or is not division of labor and social cooperation and whether society is organized on the basis of private or of public control of the means of production, originary interest is always present. In a socialist commonwealth its role would not differ from that in the market economy.

Böhm-Bawerk has once for all unmasked the fallacies of the naïve productivity explanations of interest, i.e., of the idea that interest is the expression of the physical productivity of factors of production. However, Böhm-Bawerk has himself based his own theory to some extent on the productivity approach. In referring in his explanation to the technological superiority of more time-consuming, roundabout processes of production, he avoids the crudity of the naïve productivity fallacies. But in fact he returns, although in a subtler form, to the productivity approach. Those later economists who, neglecting the time-preference idea, have stressed exclusively the productivity idea contained in Böhm-Bawerk's theory cannot help concluding that originary interest must disappear if men were one day to reach a state of affairs in which no further lengthening of the period of production could bring about a further increase in productivity.[2] This is, however, utterly wrong. Originary interest cannot disappear as long as there is scarcity and therefore action.

As long as the world is not transformed into a land of Cockaigne, men are faced with scarcity and must act and economize; they are forced to choose between satisfaction in nearer and in remoter periods of the future because neither for the former nor for the latter can full contentment be attained. Then a change in the employment of factors of production which withdraws such factors from their employment for want-satisfaction in the nearer future and devotes them to want-satisfaction in the remoter future must necessarily impair the state of satisfaction in the nearer future and improve it in the remoter future. If we were to assume that this is not the case, we should become

---

2 Cf. F.A. Hayek, "The Mythology of Capital," *The Quarterly Journal of Economics* 50 (1936): 223ff. However Professor Hayek has since partly changed his point of view. (Cf. his article "Time-Preference and Productivity, a Reconsideration," *Economica*, n.s., 12 [1945]: 22–25). But the idea criticized in the text is still widely held by economists.

embroiled in insoluble contradictions. We may at best think of a state of affairs in which technological knowledge and skill have reached a point beyond which no further progress is possible for mortal men. No new processes increasing the output per unit of input can henceforth be invented. But if we suppose that some factors of production are scarce, we must not assume that all processes which—apart from the time they absorb—are the most productive ones are fully utilized, and that no process rendering a smaller output per unit of input is resorted to merely because of the fact that it produces its final result sooner than other, physically more productive processes. Scarcity of factors of production means that we are in a position to draft plans for the improvement of our well-being the realization of which is unfeasible because of the insufficient quantity of the means available. It is precisely the unfeasibility of such desirable improvements that constitutes the element of scarcity. The reasoning of the modern supporters of the productivity approach is misled by the connotations of Böhm-Bawerk's term *roundabout methods of production* and the idea of technological improvement which it suggests. However, if there is scarcity, there must always be an unused technological opportunity to improve the state of well-being by a lengthening of the period of production in some branches of industry, regardless of whether or not the state of technological knowledge has changed. If the means are scarce, if the praxeological correlation of ends and means still exists, there are by logical necessity unsatisfied wants with regard both to nearer and to remoter periods of the future. There are always goods the procurement of which we must forego because the way that leads to their production is too long and would prevent us from satisfying more urgent needs. The fact that we do not provide more amply for the future is the outcome of a weighing of satisfaction in nearer periods of the future against satisfaction in remoter periods of the future. The ratio which is the outcome of this valuation is originary interest.

In such a world of perfect technological knowledge a promoter drafts a plan *A* according to which a hotel in picturesque, but not easily accessible, mountain districts and the roads leading to it should be built. In examining the practicability of this plan he discovers that the means available are not sufficient for its execution. Calculating the prospects of the profitability of the investment, he comes to the conclusion that the expected proceeds are not great enough to cover the costs of material and labor to be expended and interest on the capital to be invested. He renounces the execution of project A and embarks instead upon the realization of another plan, B. According to plan B the hotel is to be erected in a more easily accessible location which does not offer all the advantages of the picturesque landscape which plan A had selected, but in which it can be built either with lower costs of construction or finished in a shorter time. If no interest on the capital invested were to enter into the calculation, the illusion could arise that the state of the market data—supply of capital goods and the valuations of the public—allows for the execution of plan A. However, the realization of plan A would withdraw scarce factors of production from employments in which they could satisfy wants considered more urgent by the consumers. It would mean a manifest malinvestment, a squandering of the means available.

A lengthening of the period of production can increase the quantity of output per unit of input or produce goods which cannot be produced at all within a shorter period of production. But it is not true that the imputation of the value of this additional wealth to the capital goods required for the lengthening of the period of production generates interest. If one were to assume this, one would relapse into the crassest errors of the productivity approach, irrefutably exploded by Böhm-Bawerk. The contribution of the complementary factors of production to the result of the process is the reason for their being considered as valuable; it explains the prices paid for them and is fully taken into account in the determination of these prices. No residuum is left that is not accounted for and could explain interest.

It has been asserted that in the imaginary construction of the evenly rotating economy no interest would appear.[3] However, it can be shown that this assertion is incompatible with the assumptions on which the construction of the evenly rotating economy is based.

We begin with the distinction between two classes of saving: plain saving and capitalist saving. Plain saving is merely the piling up of consumers' goods for later consumption. Capitalist saving is the accumulation of goods which are designed for an improvement of production processes. The aim of plain saving is later consumption; it is merely postponement of consumption. Sooner or later the goods accumulated will be consumed and nothing will be left. The aim of capitalist saving is first an improvement in the productivity of effort. It accumulates capital goods which are employed for further production and are not merely reserves for later consumption. The boon derived from plain saving is later consumption of the stock not instantly consumed but accumulated for later use. The boon derived from capitalist saving is the increase of the quantity of goods produced or the production of goods which could not be produced at all without its aid. In constructing the image of an evenly rotating (static) economy, economists disregard the process of capital accumulation; the capital goods are given and remain, as, according to the underlying assumptions, no changes occur in the data. There is neither accumulation of new capital through saving, nor consumption of capital available through a surplus of consumption over income, i.e., current production minus the funds required for the maintenance of capital. It is now our task to demonstrate that these assumptions are incompatible with the idea that there is no interest.

There is no need to dwell, in this reasoning, upon plain saving. The objective of plain saving is to provide for a future in

---

[3] Cf. Joseph Schumpeter, *The Theory of Economic Development*, R. Opie, trans. (Cambridge, Mass.: Harvard University Press, 1934), pp. 34–46, 54.

which the saver could possibly be less amply supplied than in the present. Yet, one of the fundamental assumptions characterizing the imaginary construction of the evenly rotating economy is that the future does not differ at all from the present, that the actors are fully aware of this fact and act accordingly. Hence, in the frame of this construction, no room is left for the phenomenon of plain saving.

It is different with the fruit of capitalist saving, the accumulated stock of capital goods. There is in the evenly rotating economy neither saving and accumulation of additional capital goods nor eating up of already existing capital goods. Both phenomena would amount to a change in the data and would thus disturb the even rotation of the imaginary system. Now, the magnitude of saving and capital accumulation in the past—i.e., in the period preceding the establishment of the evenly rotating economy—was adjusted to the height of the rate of interest. If—with the establishment of the conditions of the evenly rotating economy—the owners of the capital goods were no longer to receive any interest, the conditions which were operative in the allocation of the available stocks of goods to the satisfaction of wants in the various periods of the future would be upset. The altered state of affairs requires a new allocation. Also in the evenly rotating economy the difference in the valuation of want-satisfaction in various periods of the future cannot disappear. Also in the frame of this imaginary construction, people will assign a higher value to an apple available today as against an apple available in ten or a hundred years. If the capitalist no longer receives interest, the balance between satisfaction in nearer and remoter periods of the future is disarranged. The fact that a capitalist has maintained his capital at just 100,000 dollars was conditioned by the fact that 100,000 present dollars were equal to 105,000 dollars available twelve months later. These 5,000 dollars were in his eyes sufficient to outweigh the advantages to be expected from an instantaneous consumption of a part of this sum. If interest payments are eliminated, capital consumption ensues.

This is the essential deficiency of the static system as Schumpeter depicts it. It is not sufficient to assume that the capital equipment of such a system has been accumulated in the past, that it is now available to the extent of this previous accumulation and is henceforth unalterably maintained at this level. We must also assign in the frame of this imaginary system a role to the operation of forces which bring about such a maintenance. If one eliminates the capitalist's role as receiver of interest, one replaces it by the capitalist's role as consumer of capital. There is no longer any reason why the owner of capital goods should abstain from employing them for consumption. Under the assumptions implied in the imaginary construction of static conditions (the evenly rotating economy) there is no need to keep them in reserve for rainy days. But even if, inconsistently enough, we were to assume that a part of them is devoted to this purpose and therefore withheld from current consumption, at least that part of capital will be consumed which corresponds to the amount that capitalist saving exceeds plain saving.[4]

If there were no originary interest, capital goods would not be devoted to immediate consumption and capital would not be consumed. On the contrary, under such an unthinkable and unimaginable state of affairs there would be no consumption at all, but only saving, accumulation of capital, and investment. Not the impossible disappearance of originary interest, but the abolition of payment of interest to the owners of capital, would result in capital consumption. The capitalists would consume their capital goods and their capital precisely because there is originary interest and present want-satisfaction is preferred to later satisfaction.

Therefore there cannot be any question of abolishing interest by any institutions, laws, and devices of bank manipulation. He who wants to "abolish" interest will have to induce people to value an apple available in a hundred years no less than a present

---

[4] Cf. Lionel Robbins, "On a Certain Ambiguity in the Conception of Stationary Equilibrium," *The Economic Journal* 40 (1930): 211ff.

apple. What can be abolished by laws and decrees is merely the right of the capitalists to receive interest. But such laws would bring about capital consumption and would very soon throw mankind back into the original state of natural poverty.

The Height of Interest Rates

In plain saving and in the capitalist saving of isolated economic actors the difference in the valuation of want satisfaction in various periods of the future manifests itself in the extent to which people provide in a more ample way for nearer than for remoter periods of the future. Under the conditions of a market economy the rate of originary interest is, provided the assumptions involved in the imaginary construction of the evenly rotating economy are present, equal to the ratio of a definite amount of money available today and the amount available at a later date which is considered as its equivalent.

The rate of originary interest directs the investment activities of the entrepreneurs. It determines the length of waiting time and of the period of production in every branch of industry.

People often raise the question of which rate of interest, a "high" or a "low," stimulates saving and capital accumulation more and which less. The question makes no sense. The lower the discount attached to future goods is, the lower is the rate of originary interest. People do not save more because the rate of originary interest rises, and the rate of originary interest does not drop on account of an increase in the amount of saving. Changes in the originary rates of interest and in the amount of saving are—other things, especially the institutional conditions, being equal—two aspects of the same phenomenon. The disappearance of originary interest would be tantamount to the disappearance of consumption. The increase of originary interest beyond all measure would be tantamount to the disappearance of saving and any provision for the future.

The quantity of the available supply of capital goods influences neither the rate of originary interest nor the amount of further saving. Even the most plentiful supply of capital need not necessarily bring about either a lowering of the rate of originary interest or a drop in the propensity to save. The increase in capital accumulation and the per capita quota of capital invested which is a characteristic mark of economically advanced nations does not necessarily either lower the rate of originary interest or weaken the propensity of individuals to make additional savings. People are, in dealing with these problems, for the most part misled by comparing merely the market rates of interest as they are determined on the loan market. However, these gross rates are not merely expressive of the height of originary interest. They contain, as will be shown later, other elements besides, the effect of which accounts for the fact that the gross rates are as a rule higher in poorer countries than in richer ones.

It is generally asserted that, other things being equal, the better individuals are supplied for the immediate future, the better they provide for wants for the remoter future. Consequently, it is said, the amount of total saving and capital accumulation within an economic system depends on the arrangement of the population into groups of different income levels. In a society with approximate income equality there is, it is said, less saving than in a society in which there is more inequality. There is a grain of truth in such observations. However, they are statements about psychological facts and as such lack the universal validity and necessity inherent in praxeological statements. Moreover, the other things the equality of which they presuppose comprehend the various individuals' valuations, their subjective value judgments in weighing the pros and cons of immediate consumption and of postponement of consumption. There are certainly many individuals whose behavior they describe correctly, but there also are other individuals who act in a different way. The French peasants, although for the most part people of moderate wealth and income, were in the nineteenth century widely known for their parsimonious habits, while the wealthy members of the aristocracy and the heirs of huge fortunes amassed in commerce and industry were no less renowned for their profligacy.

It is therefore impossible to formulate any praxeological theorem concerning the relation of the amount of capital available in the whole nation or to individual people on the one hand and the amount of saving or capital consumption and the height of the originary rate of interest on the other hand. The allocation of scarce resources to want satisfaction in various periods of the future is determined by value judgments and indirectly by all those factors which constitute the individuality of the acting man.

Originary Interest in the Changing Economy

So far we have dealt with the problem of originary interest under certain assumptions: that the turnover of goods is effected by the employment of neutral money; that saving, capital accumulation, and the determination of interest rates are not hampered by institutional obstacles; and that the whole economic process goes on in the frame of an evenly rotating economy. We shall eliminate the first two of these assumptions in the following chapter.[5] Now we want to deal with originary interest in a changing economy.

He who wants to provide for the satisfaction of future needs must correctly anticipate these needs. If he fails in this understanding of the future, his provision will prove less satisfactory or totally futile. There is no such thing as an abstract saving that could provide for all classes of want-satisfaction and would be neutral with regard to changes occurring in conditions and valuations. Originary interest can therefore in the changing economy never appear in a pure unalloyed form. It is only in the imaginary construction of the evenly rotating economy that the mere passing of time matures originary interest; in the passage of time and with the progress of the process of production more and more value accrues, as it were, to the complementary factors

---

5 [See Ludwig von Mises, "Interest, Credit Expansion, and the Trade Cycle," in *Human Action: A Treatise on Economics* (Auburn, Ala.: Ludwig von Mises Institute, 1998), pp. 535–83.]

of production; with the termination of the process of production the lapse of time has generated in the price of the product the full quota of originary interest. In the changing economy during the period of production there also arise synchronously other changes in valuations. Some goods are valued higher than previously, some lower. These alterations are the source from which entrepreneurial profits and losses stem. Only those entrepreneurs who in their planning have correctly anticipated the future state of the market are in a position to reap, in selling the products, an excess over the costs of production (inclusive of net originary interest) expended. An entrepreneur who has failed in his speculative understanding of the future can sell his products, if at all, only at prices which do not cover completely his expenditures plus originary interest on the capital invested.

Like entrepreneurial profit and loss, interest is not a price, but a magnitude which is to be disengaged by a particular mode of computation from the price of the products of successful business operations. The gross difference between the price at which a commodity is sold and the costs expended in its production (exclusive of interest on the capital invested) was called profit in the terminology of British classical economics.[6] Modern economics conceives this magnitude as a complex of catallactically disparate items. The excess of gross receipts over expenditures which the classical economists called profit includes the price for the entrepreneur's own labor employed in the process of production, interest on the capital invested, and finally entrepreneurial profit proper. If such an excess has not been reaped at all in the sale of the products, the entrepreneur not only fails to get profit proper, he receives neither an equivalent for the market value of the labor he has contributed nor interest on the capital invested.

---

6 Cf. Richard Whately, *Elements of Logic*, 9th ed. (London: J.W. Parker, 1848), pp. 354ff.; Edwin Cannan, *A History of the Theories of Production and Distribution in English Political Economy from 1776 to 1848*, 3rd ed. (London: P.S. King, 1924), pp. 189ff.

The breaking down of gross profit (in the classical sense of the term) into managerial wages, interest, and entrepreneurial profit is not merely a device of economic theory. It developed, with progressing perfection in business practices of accountancy and calculation, in the field of commercial routine independently of the reasoning of the economists. The judicious and sensible businessman does not attach practical significance to the confused and garbled concept of profit as employed by the classical economists. His notion of costs of production includes the potential market price of his own services contributed, the interest paid on capital borrowed, and the potential interest he could earn, according to the conditions of the market, on his own capital invested in the enterprise by lending it to other people. Only the excess of proceeds over the costs so calculated is in his eyes entrepreneurial profit.[7]

The precipitation of entrepreneurial wages from the complex of all the other items included in the profit concept of classical economics presents no particular problem. It is more difficult to sunder entrepreneurial profit from originary interest. In the changing economy interest stipulated in loan contracts is always a gross magnitude out of which the pure rate of originary interest must be computed by a particular process of computation and analytical repartition. It has been shown already that in every act of lending, even apart from the problem of changes in the monetary unit's purchasing power, there is an element of entrepreneurial venture. The granting of credit is necessarily always an entrepreneurial speculation which can possibly result in failure and the loss of a part or of the total amount lent. Every interest stipulated and paid in loans includes not only originary interest but also entrepreneurial profit.

This fact for a long time misled the attempts to construct a satisfactory theory of interest. It was only the elaboration of the imaginary construction of the evenly rotating economy that

---

[7] But, of course, the present-day intentional confusion of all economic concepts is conducive to obscuring this distinction. Thus, in the United States, in dealing with the dividends paid by corporations people speak of "profits."

made it possible to distinguish precisely between originary interest and entrepreneurial profit and loss.

The Computation of Interest

Originary interest is the outgrowth of valuations unceasingly fluctuating and changing. It fluctuates and changes with them. The custom of computing interest pro anno is merely commercial usage and a convenient rule of reckoning. It does not affect the height of the interest rates as determined by the market.

The activities of the entrepreneurs tend toward the establishment of a uniform rate of originary interest in the whole market economy. If there turns up in one sector of the market a margin between the prices of present goods and those of future goods which deviates from the margin prevailing in other sectors, a trend toward equalization is brought about by the striving of businessmen to enter those sectors in which this margin is higher and to avoid those in which it is lower. The final rate of originary interest is the same in all parts of the market of the evenly rotating economy.

The valuations resulting in the emergence of originary interest prefer satisfaction in a nearer period of the future to satisfaction of the same kind and extent in a remoter period of the future. Nothing would justify the assumption that this discounting of satisfaction in remoter periods progresses continuously and evenly. If we were to assume this, we would imply that the period of provision is infinite. However, the mere fact that individuals differ in their provision for future needs and that even to the most provident actor provision beyond a definite period appears supererogatory, forbids us to think of the period of provision as infinite.

The usages of the loan market must not mislead us. It is customary to stipulate a uniform rate of interest for the whole duration of a loan contract[8] and to apply a uniform rate in computing compound interest. The real determination of interest

---

8 There are, of course, also deviations from this usage.

rates is independent of these and other arithmetical devices of interest computation. If the rate of interest is unalterably fixed by contract for a period of time, intervening changes in the market rate of interest are reflected in corresponding changes in the prices paid for the principal, due allowance being made for the fact that the amount of principal to be paid back at the maturity of the loan is unalterably stipulated. It does not affect the result whether one calculates with an unchanging rate of interest and changing prices of the principal or with changing interest rates and an unchanging amount of the principal, or with changes in both magnitudes.

The terms of a loan contract are not independent of the stipulated duration of the loan. Not only because those components of the gross rate of market interest which made it deviate from the rate of originary interest are affected by differences in the duration of the loan, but also on account of factors which bring about changes in the rate of originary interest, loan contracts are valued and appraised differently according to the duration of the loan stipulated.

In Defense of the Misesian Theory of Interest

{ *By Roger W. Garrison* }

Introduction

The recently published volume, *New Directions in Austrian Economics*,[1] consists of the papers presented at a conference held in September 1976 at Windsor Castle, England. Each paper was followed by two formal critiques. Original publication plans provided for the inclusion of these critiques, but subsequent editorial decisions resulted in the publication of the papers only.

The present article is a slightly expanded version of one of the critiques of Professor Laurence S. Moss's paper directed against the theory of interest of Ludwig von Mises. As a means of abstraction, Moss discussed the economics of a pure exchange economy in terms of the allocation of consumer goods over time in a prisoner-of-war camp. His paper is thoroughly neoclassical rather than Austrian in substance and in form, and hence does not do justice to Mises's theory of interest, which was developed within the context of his own praxeological framework of analysis. The extent of this injustice is pointed out in the present paper.

Reprinted from the *Journal of Libertarian Studies* 3, no. 2 (1979).

[1] Louis M. Spadaro, ed., *New Directions in Austrian Economics* (Kansas City: Sheed Andrews and McMeel, 1978).

The following critical comments were originally intended primarily for those who had read Moss's paper. Even standing alone, however, this critique can give the reader a feel for the fundamental differences between neoclassical and Austrian theory—differences that are not at all made evident in Moss's paper.

It is encouraging that some present-day economists schooled in the neoclassical tradition are interested in "new directions." But the Moss paper starkly points up the fact that if they wish to embark on new directions in *Austrian* economics, they had better adopt the Austrian tradition as their point of origin.

Moss's Critique of Mises

In his paper, "The Emergence of Interest in a Pure Exchange Economy: Notes on a Theorem Attributed to Ludwig von Mises," Moss is concerned with two aspects of Mises's theory of interest. He is concerned with the contentions that (1) "Misesian time preference guarantees the emergence of a positive rate of interest in a pure exchange economy," and that (2) this positive rate "results entirely from the interaction of valuing minds and is therefore a subjective phenomenon."[2] As a means of evaluating these two contentions, Moss offers us "a model of a pure exchange economy with an analysis of the circumstances under which a positive market rate of interest will emerge." Ultimately, he arrives at two conclusions: (1) that the emergence of a positive rate is not "guaranteed" by time preference alone, but depends, in part, on the existence of certain conditions, and (2) that because these conditions are objective in nature, Mises's theory of interest cannot be said to be a purely subjective theory.[3]

If these two conclusions are correct, then Misesian interest theory differs from neoclassical interest theory only in trivial respects. A casual reading of Moss's paper leaves one with the

---

2 Laurence S. Moss, "The Emergence of Interest in a Pure Exchange Economy: Notes on a Theorem Attributed to Ludwig von Mises," in Spadaro, *New Directions*, p. 157.

3 Ibid., pp. 163–64.

impression that the only difference is that Mises was somewhat confused about the meaning of the term *time preference*. I will argue in what follows that this impression is the result of looking at Misesian theory through neoclassical glasses, and that on removing those glasses both of Moss's conclusions will be seen to be highly misleading, if not wholly mistaken.

Time Preference: Neoclassical and Misesian

Moss sets out to show us "that much of the misunderstanding regarding Mises's interest theory has to do with the special meaning Mises attached to the term *time preference*."[4] He establishes that Mises and the neoclassicals (Fisher, Becker) do in fact use this term to mean different things, but he stops just short of identifying the ultimate source and the fundamental nature of the difference. Instead, Moss attributes the misunderstanding to "semantic considerations" and claims that with regard to the concept of time preference, "there is no fundamental issue separating Mises from the remainder of the economics profession."[5] But the difference is every bit as fundamental as the difference between praxeology—Mises's approach to economic theory—and the "pure logic of choice" associated with neoclassical theory. In fact, the concept of time preference can serve to illustrate the nature of these two basically different approaches to the study of economics.

The neoclassicals define the concept in terms of the time pattern of consumption preferred by the individual. An individual who prefers a uniform distribution of consumption over time, over all other possible distributions, is characterized as having a neutral or zero time preference. Individuals who prefer to consume relatively more now or in the near future, and those who prefer to consume relatively more in the more remote future, are characterized as having positive and negative time preferences respectively. To make these characteristics "operationally

---

4 Moss, "Emergence of Interest," p. 158.
5 Ibid., p. 162.

meaningful" the consumption patterns are expressed in terms of units of some homogeneous consumption good. (In Moss's discussion, for example, neutral time preference describes a prisoner of war who is "satisfied with an equal number of apples in each time period."[6]) The use of the single homogeneous consumption good allows the alternative consumption patterns to be expressed in objective and measurable terms. And the utility that an individual would derive from the various consumption patterns can be written as a "function" of the number of apples consumed in each period. With this formulation any individual's most-preferred pattern can be determined by solving a standard constrained-maximization problem. The individual's utility (Moss's Eq. 1) is maximized subject to his budget constraint (Moss's Eq. 3). The result is Moss's Eq. 2. The distribution of apple consumption can then be subjected to the litmus test, that is, it can be compared to a uniform distribution of apple consumption to determine whether the individual's time preference is positive, negative or neutral. The only problem with this procedure, in the eyes of the neoclassicals, is the possibility of an ambiguous litmus test. Unless the preferred distribution is monotonically non-increasing or monotonically non-decreasing over time (to use the neoclassical jargon) the test may fail. This problem is akin to the notorious "re-switching" controversy that has plagued neoclassical capital theorists for the past several decades.

Mises's treatment of time-preference theory is fundamentally different from that of the neoclassicals. Moss points out that "[a]ccording to Mises, the very act of consuming during the planning period demonstrates (positive) time preference," and that "[s]ince any [consumption pattern] is evidence of what Mises called 'time preference,' he must have meant by the term something different from what has become standard terminology among neoclassical economists."[7] But Moss wrongly attributes the difference to semantic considerations. Mises's theory was

---

6 Moss, "Emergence of Interest," p. 161.
7 Ibid.

formulated not in terms of consumption goods or patterns of consumption, but rather in terms of *action*. That is, his time-preference theory is a praxeological theory. For Mises the *act* of consuming is evidence of time preference because action per se is evidence of time preference. By acting now the individual reveals that such is preferred to deferring action, and as all acts are ultimately directed at achieving consumption, the individual reveals a preference for consumption in the nearer future to consumption in the more remote future. This is Mises's time-preference theorem. In his own words: "[W]hoever seeks by acting to relieve a felt uneasiness is always expressing a preference for earlier over later satisfaction."[8]

Misesian time-preference theory, having been formulated in terms of actions, can be *applied* to the category of goods. Noting that Mises included nonmaterial goods (i.e., services) in his concept of goods,[9] it can be said that all action is directed toward the acquisition of goods. Any particular actions taken by an individual will be associated (in the mind of the acting individual) with particular goods. By his acting, then, he reveals a preference for acquiring these goods at an earlier point in the future over acquiring them at a more remote point in the future. This holds true whether the actions consist of gathering goods, bargaining with another individual for goods, or producing goods.

It should be clear now that the difference between the neoclassical and the Misesian formulations is a fundamental and not just a semantic difference. It should be equally clear that Moss's suggestion that by time preference Mises really meant "time allocation"[10] would serve only to obscure this difference and to compound rather than dispel the confusion surrounding

---

8 Ludwig von Mises, "A Critique of Böhm-Bawerk's Reasoning in Support of his Time Preference Theory," in Percy L. Greaves, Jr., *Mises Made Easier* (New York: Free Market Books, 1974), p. 156. Also, for similar statements see Mises, *Human Action: A Treatise on Economics*, 3rd rev. ed. (Chicago: Henry Regnery Co., 1966), pp. 483–90.
9 Mises, *Human Action*, p. 94.
10 Spadaro, *New Directions*, p. 161.

the issue. It is the neoclassicals who are concerned with time allocation and with comparing different time patterns of consumption with a uniform pattern. This has no place in Mises's praxeological formulation. Firstly, the notion of a uniform pattern of consumption, outside the context of a one-commodity world, has no clear-cut and unambiguous meaning.[11] Second, there is no logical or necessary connection between an individual's actions and his notions about what constitutes a uniform pattern of consumption. Mises's theory is derived from the fact that man *acts*, and is independent of the particular pattern of consumption that may result from his acting.

Intertemporal Exchange and Internal Financing

Moss couches his argument in terms of the economics of a prisoner-of-war camp and considers the nature of intertemporal exchange under two different institutional arrangements. "Internal financing"[12]—a term whose meaning will shortly become apparent—is allowed in the first case he considers, but is precluded in the second. This section will deal with the case in which "internal financing" is allowed.

Mossian Apples and Fisherian Hardtack

In order to abstract from the heterogeneity of consumption goods and all the associated problems and ambiguities, Moss envisions a prisoner-of-war camp in which apples are the only consumption good. Each prisoner is to receive a fixed number of apples over a certain period of time. The time pattern of apple delivery is known to the prisoners in advance. Moss assumes throughout his discussion that storage costs are zero,[13] that the apples

---

[11] On the difficulties of the notion of a uniform pattern of consumption see Israel M. Kirzner, *An Essay on Capital* (New York: Augustus M. Kelley Publishers, 1966), pp. 68–71. Also F.A. Hayek, *The Pure Theory of Capital* (Chicago: University of Chicago Press, 1941), p. 159.

[12] Spadaro, *New Directions*, p. 158.

[13] Ibid., p. 159.

do not spoil, and that there is no possibility of theft or accidental destruction.[14] Initially, Moss supposes that each prisoner is given the option of transferring apples promised in more remote consumption periods to periods more proximate simply by so requesting.[15] (This is the "internal financing.") But given this option together with Moss's assumptions it should be obvious that receiving the entire stock of apples at the outset would be as preferred or preferable to any other delivery scheme. The multi-period prisoner-of-war camp scenario with its preset delivery schedule, coupled with an allowance for internal financing, is thus reduced to a scenario in which an individual finds himself with nothing but a fixed quantity of an indestructible consumption good. This situation is identical to the one envisioned by Irving Fisher in his notorious "hardtack" illustration.[16] Fisher imagined a group of sailors shipwrecked on a desert island with nothing but 100,000 pounds of "hardtack." (Hardtack is a very hard marginally edible biscuit made of flour and water without salt.) "A little reflection will show," Fisher tells us, "that in such a [situation] the rate of interest *in terms of hardtack* would necessarily be zero."[17] Similarly, Moss's discussion indicates that with internal financing allowed, the rate of interest *in terms of apples* would necessarily be zero.[18]

The Mossian apples are logically equivalent to Fisherian hardtack. The reasoning applied to both scenarios can be understood in terms of the neoclassical orthodoxy. Neoclassical theory focuses on the physical good itself, and on the (technologically determined) rate of transformation of a unit of the good today into a unit of the good tomorrow. While the mere passage of time will transform one piece of hardtack (or one apple) today into one piece of hardtack (or one apple) tomorrow, no other (more

---

14 Spadaro, *New Directions*, p. 165.
15 Ibid., p. 159.
16 Irving Fisher, *The Theory of Interest: As Determined by Impatience to Spend Income and Opportunity to Invest It* (New York: Macmillan, 1930), pp. 186–91.
17 Ibid., p. 186. Emphasis in original.
18 Spadaro, *New Directions*, p. 162.

productive) intertemporal transformations are possible. Therefore, the rate of interest is zero. This conclusion seems to follow almost in independence of the existence of shipwrecked sailors or prisoners of war.

Neither scenario makes much sense in terms of Misesian theory, which focuses not on the goods themselves, but on the actions of individuals. (This is why it is important to rid Moss's scenario of the extraneous "actions" associated with periodic apple deliveries and internal financing.) Granted, in either of these scenarios where the individuals can only live a hand-to-mouth existence, there simply isn't much action. And to this extent the praxeologist has nothing of great importance to say. But what little action there is *does* reveal time preference in the Misesian sense. A piece of hardtack in the hand is revealed to be preferred to a piece of hardtack lying on the ground, and a piece of hardtack in the mouth is revealed to be preferred to a piece of hardtack in the hand. These revealed preferences imply value differentials between hardtack on the ground, in the hand, and in the mouth. But the value differentials will not give rise to an intertemporal market. That is, in Fisher's and Moss's scenarios there is no room for interpersonal exchanges: There are no market prices. There is no market rate of interest. There is no market. The shipwrecked sailors are engaging in what Mises termed "autistic exchange." They are foregoing leisure in order to consume hardtack. It may seem trivial to point all this out, but the triviality should be attributed to the scenarios themselves and not to Mises's theory. If the plight of the shipwrecked sailors were truly the plight of mankind, Mises no doubt would not have bothered to formulate his time-preference theory of interest. Instead he would have spent his ninety-two years devouring hardtack along with the rest of us. But such is not the plight of mankind. In a market economy man's actions, far from being trivial, are of great significance to the economic theorist. The diverse actions of market participants reveal their time preferences, which in turn imply value differentials between the objects of their actions, and these value differentials are expressed in the intertemporal market as a positive rate of interest.

Fisherian Figs

Throughout Moss's discussion the assumption that the apples do not spoil is never relaxed. Presumably, had he allowed for spoilage he would have had to conclude that a negative rate of interest is possible. Thus, the notion of a negative rate attributable to the spoiling of the one and only consumption good deserves some comment here. Fisher held that negative interest is possible, and to illustrate the possibility he modified his shipwrecked-sailor scenario, replacing the indestructible hardtack with rotting figs.[19] Again, Fisher focused on the figs themselves and couched his argument in terms of the (technologically determined) rate of transformation between figs today and figs tomorrow. The deterioration of the figs was assumed to proceed at a fixed and foreknown rate of 50 percent per annum. After stating this assumed rate of physical deterioration, Fisher leaped to the conclusion that the rate of interest in terms of figs would necessarily be minus 50 percent.[20] This is his conclusion in spite of the fact that (as Fisher himself recognized) there would be no intertemporal (or interpersonal) market for figs. His negative rate of interest is virtually independent of the plans and actions of the shipwrecked sailors. The absurdity of the notion of an interest rate divorced from an intertemporal market and from the actions of market participants can be demonstrated by applying Fisher's reasoning to other technologically determined rates. Suppose there are no figs at all on the desert island and that the island itself is washing away into the sea at the rate of 20 percent per annum. Would the rate of interest in terms of the island be minus 20 percent? Or suppose the sailors themselves were losing weight due to malnutrition at the rate of 30 percent per annum. Would the interest rate in terms of the sailors be minus

---

19 Fisher, *Theory of Interest*, pp. 191–92.
20 Ibid., p. 191.

30 percent? If it is the physical characteristics of reality rather than the "interaction of valuing minds" that determine the rate of interest, it would be difficult not to answer these questions in the affirmative. Of course, all that need be recognized here is that *all* rates are not rates of interest.

The praxeologist's analysis would be little affected by the substitution of rotting figs for indestructible hardtack. The sailors would still be doomed to living a hand-to-mouth existence. If anything, their time preferences would be higher now since their rotting food supply would cause their world to come to an end sooner.[21] But there would still be no intertemporal market and hence no market rate of interest.

Storage, Theft, and Accidental Destruction

The allowance for spoilage even in a one-commodity world does not imply a negative rate of interest. Nor is a negative rate implied by the relaxation of Moss's other assumptions. While it is perfectly acceptable to make the simplifying assumptions that storage and the prevention of theft and accidental destruction are costless, the impression that these assumptions are necessary to preclude the possibility of a negative rate of interest must be avoided. But the neoclassical formulation of interest theory leaves just this impression. One modern author writes: "The interest rate [in a one-commodity world] can be ... negative," but "[n]o lender will pay more interest to a borrower than it would cost to store the [commodity]."[22] While it is true that the payment for storage may be larger than the implicit interest payment, this payment *when understood in terms of the individual's plans and actions* is conceptually distinct from the payment of interest. That is, payment for storage should not be treated analytically as a *component* of the interest rate. Similarly, intertemporal transactions that are motivated by the desire to prevent theft or accidental destruction should be analyzed as such. In transactions of this

---

21 See Murray N. Rothbard, *Man, Economy, and State: A Treatise on Economic Principles*, 2 vols. (Los Angeles: Nash, 1971), pp. 380–81.
22 George J. Stigler, *The Theory of Price*, 3rd ed. (New York: Macmillan, 1966), p. 278.

sort the individual "lender" is, from his own perspective, purchasing theft-prevention or accident-prevention services. The payment for these preventative services must be kept conceptually distinct from the payment of interest. These important conceptual distinctions are virtually impossible to maintain, though, unless the focus of the analysis is on the plans and actions of the individual market participants, rather than on the physical goods themselves. In the Misesian theory of interest the distinction is obvious; in the neoclassical theory it is hopelessly obscured.

Internal Financing Disallowed

After concluding in straightforward neoclassical fashion that a zero rate of interest would prevail in a prisoner-of-war camp where internal financing is allowed, Moss moves on to analyze the more relevant situation. The prisoners no longer have the option of simply requesting the delivery now of apples scheduled for delivery at a future date. That is, if an individual prisoner wants to consume more apples than he now has, he cannot internally finance his consumption deficit, but must engage instead in intertemporal exchange with his fellow prisoners. Of course, if he wants to consume fewer apples than he now has, he can (costlessly) carry his surplus of apples forward in time. In this new situation where internal financing is disallowed "present goods can be costlessly transferred into the future but future goods cannot be conjured into the present." "Time," to use Moss's metaphor, "is a one-way street."[23] Moss observes that it is this "asymmetry in the time market" that gives rise to the possibility of intertemporal exchange and a positive rate of interest.

I have no quarrel with Moss's reasoning to this point. In fact, strong support can be found for it in the writings of the Austrian capital theorists. In 1956, for instance, Professor Lachmann pointed out that "the ultimate reason [that the rate of interest cannot be negative] lies in the simple fact that stocks of goods can

---

23 Spadaro, *New Directions*, p. 164.

be carried forward in time but not backwards."[24] Moss appears to be on solid ground. But his purpose here is not to show that the rate of interest must be positive but rather to show that Mises's theory of interest is not a purely subjective theory. It is in his attempt to demonstrate this that Moss has seriously erred.

The source of the error is the confusion of subjectivity in value theory with subjectivity in metaphysics. Moss is obviously referring to his observation about the nature of time when he says that "the emergence of interest ... depends in part on the existence of certain *objective* conditions."[25] This "objectivity," however, lies completely outside the domain of value theory, and is properly the subject matter of metaphysics. That Moss is dealing with a metaphysical issue here is somewhat obscured by his use of the prisoner-of-war-camp scenario with internal financing first allowed and then disallowed. We don't normally think of the rationing policy in a prisoner-of-war camp as a metaphysical issue. But in the context of Moss's discussion it is just that. This is clearly recognized in Radford's classic account of the economics of a prisoner-of-war camp which serves as a basis for Moss's scenario. Radford tells us that the Red Cross which was dispensing the supplies "may be considered as 'Nature' of the textbooks, and the articles of trade—food, clothing and cigarettes—as free gifts—land or manna."[26]

Moss is clearly arguing in metaphysical terms, though, in his final paragraph where he writes of "a world where the present gradually unfolds into the future rather than the other way around."[27] Recognizing that this is the way the world really is, Moss concludes that "Mises's attempt to present a purely subjective time-preference ... theory of interest must at the very least admit the empirical or broadly technological assumption

---

24 Ludwig M. Lachmann, *Capital and Its Structure* (London: London School of Economics, 1956), p. 78.
25 Spadaro, *New Directions*, p. 158. Emphasis added.
26 R.A. Radford, "The Economic Organization of a P.O.W. Camp," *Economica*, n.s., 12 (November, 1945): 192–93.
27 Spadaro, *New Directions*, p. 164.

that the transfer of goods through time is indeed a one-way street."[28] We can be confident, however, that Mises would never have considered this (or any other) aspect of the nature of time to be an assumption in the sense that Moss's paper suggests. He would have recognized it instead as a fundamental metaphysical relationship, and would have been happy to "admit" that not only his theory of interest but, more generally, his theory of value presupposes that metaphysical relationships are what they are. This is not an admission that Mises's theory of interest is not a purely subjective theory, however, for the simple reason that subjectivism in value theory does not imply or require subjectivism in metaphysics.

Moss's criticism of Mises couched in terms of a particular aspect of Mises's value theory and a particular metaphysical relationship may appear to have some plausibility. The fallacy becomes more apparent, though, when the criticism is generalized:

> Subjective value theory presupposes existence.
> Existence is objective.
> So much for subjective value theory.

This is in essence what Moss is saying, and again the error is in the mixing of value theory and metaphysics. Mises's pure time-preference theory of interest is not inconsistent with the recognition of (an objective) existence. Mises was *not* a solipsist; he *was* a thoroughgoing subjective-value theorist.

Concluding Remarks

I have attempted to criticize Moss's paper from a Misesian perspective. I would have given him a higher mark had he more fully presented Mises's position that a positive rate of interest will emerge even in a pure exchange economy, related it to Mises's general theoretical framework, and evaluated Mises's

---

28 Spadaro, *New Directions*, p. 164.

arguments in the context of that framework. But instead, Moss couched Mises's position in neoclassical terms, spelled out the conditions under which neoclassical theory would support this position, and then criticized Mises for not recognizing these conditions. Because of this approach Moss's paper helps us very little in understanding Mises's theory of interest as applied to a pure exchange economy. It does, however, help us to understand why neoclassical theorists are characteristically baffled by the Misesian theory of interest.

The Pure Time-Preference Theory of Interest: An Attempt at Clarification*

{ *By Israel M. Kirzner* }

For almost a century a particular theory of interest has been again and again discussed, refuted, defended, ignored, forgotten, and rediscovered; somehow it has managed to survive. This theory is the pure time-preference theory (often to be referred to in this paper as PTPT). For the most part this theory has, especially during the last half-century, languished as a basically discredited, definitely unfashionable, point of view. Yet the theory was never finally interred—nor did it even wholly expire. The theory is often described as Austrian, but, as we shall see, it is not the only and not the best known Austrian theory of interest. In recent decades a certain revival of discussion has emerged surrounding this pure time-preference theory (partly, no doubt, as a result of the modest revival of interest in Austrian economics generally).

Reprinted from *The Meaning of Ludwig von Mises: Contributions in Economics, Sociology, Epistemology, and Political Philosophy*, Jeffrey M. Herbener, ed. (Auburn, Ala.: Ludwig von Mises Institute, 1993).

* This paper owes much to countless discussions with Ingo Pellengahr over a two-year period. His open-minded but persistent questioning concerning troublesome aspects of PTPT helped (and compelled) the writer toward the present clarification. For Pellengahr's own perspective on the matters dealt with in this paper see references to Pellengahr.

Almost invariably, contemporary economists have reacted to renewed discussions of the pure time-preference theory with utter disbelief and plain bewilderment. These critics have found the theory simply incredible; the idea that the phenomenon of interest is in *no* way dependent upon physical productivity is one that the critics find patently absurd; that serious thinkers should accept this absurdity, they find quite incomprehensible. The present paper does not seek to argue any superiority of PTPT over its competitors in the field of interest theories. Rather we seek to dispel the bewilderment that moderns display in regard to it. This task of clarification will turn out to involve certain "philosophical," extra-economic issues that are of significance for economists in their own right, in several respects.

The Interest Problem

Much—perhaps all—will turn out to depend on the way in which the interest problem is formulated. For present purposes we adopt a modern formulation of the problem, but wish to emphasize that this formulation is very similar in spirit and character to classic formulations going back to Schumpeter[1] and Böhm-Bawerk.[2] The modern formulation we cite is that of Hausman.[3] Hausman points out than an "individual's capital ... enables that individual to earn interest. If the capital is invested in a machine, the sum of the rentals the machine earns over its lifetime is greater than the machine's cost. Why?" Common observation, that is, tells us that possession of a given stock of capital funds can, by judicious investment (say, in a machine), yield a continuous flow of income (annual rentals net of depreciation) without

---

[1] Joseph A. Schumpeter, *The Theory of Economic Development* (Cambridge, Mass.: Harvard University Press, 1934).

[2] Eugen von Böhm-Bawerk, *Capital and Interest* (Spring Mills, Penn.: Libertarian Press, 1959 [1889]). Contains translations of three volumes: vol. 1, originally published in 1884; vol. 2, originally published in 1889; vol. 3, originally published in 1921.

[3] Daniel M. Hausman, *Capital, Profits and Prices* (New York: Columbia University Press, 1981), p. 3.

impairing the ability of the capital funds to serve indefinitely as a source of income. The problem is, how this can occur. *Why is not the price of the machine* (paid by the capitalist at the time he invests in the machine) *bid up* (by the competition of others eagerly seeking to capture the net surplus of rentals over cost) *to the point where no such surplus remains?* We are seeking, then, an explanation for an observed phenomenon which is, in the absence of a theory of interest, unable to be accounted for. Absent a theory of interest, no interest income ought to be forthcoming, except as a transient phenomenon; competition ought to squeeze it out of existence.

Neoclassical theory has, in a variety of versions, seen interest as obtained and paid in return for special productive services of one kind or another. J.B. Clark and F.H. Knight saw capital as providing a flow of productive services, of which interest is the irrepressible expression. Competition does not erode it; ownership of a stock of capital inevitably confers title to a corresponding income flow. (We do not discuss, in this paper, the extent to which this theory in fact addresses the interest problem as formulated above.) For "Austrian" versions[4] of the neoclassical explanation, again, ownership of capital expresses the provision of a special productive service ("waiting") required in order to enjoy the enhanced fruits of more lengthy ("roundabout") processes of production. Competition cannot erode interest income: it *has* to be offered if potential capitalists (with positive time preference) are to be persuaded to provide the waiting (needed in order to be able to enjoy the enhanced output available through capital-using production). And, given the productivity of waiting, it *pays* to offer interest in order to elicit that waiting. In the celebrated "Cambridge Controversy" of some years back, this neoclassical view of interest was the

---

4 As we shall see, there were two "Austrian" theories of interest, both deriving from Böhm-Bawerk, see F.A. Hayek, *The Pure Theory of Capital* (London: Routledge and Kegan Paul, 1941), app. I. One of these, which (unlike Hayek) we identify with Fisher (and describe as neoclassical), is that discussed here in the text. The second is the PTPT, the subject of this paper.

only view advanced as an alternative to the neo-Ricardian perspective on interest as a surplus (to be explained, not by appeal to market exchange relations, but by "the relations between workers and capitalists including possibly their relative bargaining power").[5]

It will be useful for us to examine more carefully the above-cited "Austrian" variant of the productivity view (actually most carefully developed by Irving Fisher) in order to point up features of the alternative Austrian theory of interest, the pure time-preference theory. The pure time-preference theory (PTPT) was developed, largely from roots in Böhm-Bawerk, by Frank Fetter[6] in the United States, and later by Mises.[7] As Fetter pointed out, Böhm-Bawerk's own position appears in a number of ways to be an inconsistent one, demonstrating at some points the pure time-preference view, at other points the Fisherian physical productivity view. Let us note certain features of the Fisherian "productivity of waiting" theory.

We should note, first of all, that this theory is *not* necessarily vulnerable to the basic Böhm-Bawerkian criticism of all productivity-of-capital theories of interest. Böhm-Bawerk had criticized such theories of interest because they ignore the essential interest problem (as formulated above). It will not do to say that the machine yields interest (in the form of a flow of rentals that is greater than the cost of the machine) because the machine is physically productive. The interest problem consisted in asking why, given this physical productivity, did not the market value of the machine rise to reflect fully the rentals it is able to generate. Of course a tree produces fruit; the interest problem consists in the dilemma posed by the apparent failure of

---

5 Hausman, *Capital, Profits and Prices*, p. 167.
6 Frank A. Fetter, "The 'Roundabout Process' in the Interest Theory," *Quarterly Journal of Economics* 17 (November, 1902); reprinted in Frank Fetter, *Capital, Interest, and Rent: Essays in the Theory of Distribution*, Murray N. Rothbard, ed. (Kansas City: Sheed Andrews and McMeel, 1977). Also, Frank Fetter, "Capitalization versus Productivity: Rejoinder," *American Economic Review* (December, 1914).
7 Ludwig von Mises, *Human Action: A Treatise on Economics* (New Haven, Conn.: Yale University Press, 1949).

the market price of the tree to equal the value of the total fruit output. Simple theory tells us, after all, that the value of inputs and the value of outputs tend to equality in competitive markets.

The productivity-of-waiting theory of interest escapes this criticism by arguing that *besides* the machine, *besides* the tree, yet another "input" is required in order to command the flow of rentals (or fruit). This additional input is "waiting"; once the services of waiting are properly included in the list of needed inputs, the interest dilemma evaporates. Competition indeed squeezes out all surplus above marginal productivity returns. Interest *is*, in this view, the marginal productivity return on a scarce factor, viz., waiting.

The Fisherian "productivity-of-waiting" theory emphatically recognizes the significance of time preference. It is the circumstance of positive time preference that renders waiting a scarce, costly factor (to which interest can be attributed as a productivity return). But the interest income that might be considered the reward received by investors to induce them to provide waiting is at the same time seen as *made possible only by the productivity of waiting*. (It is in this respect, particularly, that PTPT differs from the Fisher theory. For PTPT it is incorrect to see interest income as the "fruit" of anything. Rather PTPT sees interest income as a receipt that results from the pattern of prices governing intertemporal exchanges, with these prices expressing the prevalently positive time preferences of the participants.)

As a matter of logic, the Fisher productivity-of-waiting theory deals with the interest problem (as formulated above) in impeccable manner. The only way through which the validity of the productivity-of-waiting view (at least insofar as we have presented it thus far) can be challenged is by disagreeing with the concept of "waiting" as a productive factor service. The critic may refuse to recognize that waiting (or "time") is productive, or is regarded by prospective producers as a scarce factor. The fact that an inevitable time delay must be accepted before current efforts bear fruit, need not mean that time is a necessary *ingredient* in the production process; it may simply mean that this production process is a slow one, yielding a result less valuable (in terms of anticipated attractiveness) than an otherwise similar, more speedy process.

Clearly this question of whether to treat waiting as a productive ingredient must be recognized as a strictly "philosophical" question. No economic reasoning (and certainly no amount of empirical research) can reveal whether time is (or should be treated as) itself an active productive agent or only a medium permitting the flows of inputs to cumulate into the product.[8] Moreover it is conceivable that a given observer may be prepared to recognize time as an active productive agent in some processes of production (the maturing of wine, perhaps?) while refusing to recognize it as such in other time-consuming processes of production (as, perhaps, in considering the operation of an old-fashioned, slower machine as compared with that of a faster, more modern generation of machines). In any event the relevance of the "productivity-of-waiting" theory depends *entirely* on this "philosophical" question. (Part of the dilemma posed by Böhm-Bawerk's own statement of the theory of interest was that, on the one hand, he explicitly refused to accept time or waiting as an independent factor to stand with labor and nature,[9] yet seemed on the other hand to attribute interest to the physical circumstance that roundabout processes of production are more productive. If time and waiting are not themselves to be considered productive agents, no interest could emerge as a result of the productivity of time-consuming processes of production (any more than interest can be ascribed to the fruitfulness of a tree).[10]

The basis on which the PTPT is dissatisfied with the Fisher (productivity-of-waiting) solution to the interest problem is thus strictly a non-economic "philosophic" one—viz., a view of time (and thus of waiting) that sees it (as Böhm-Bawerk himself

---

8 On this see T. Haavelmo, *A Study in the Theory of Investment* (Chicago: University of Chicago Press, 1960), p. 47; Israel M. Kirzner, *An Essay on Capital* (New York: Augustus M. Kelley, 1966), p. 97.
9 Böhm-Bawerk, *Capital and Interest*, pp. 97–98.
10 Fetter, "The 'Roundabout Process' in the Interest Theory."

apparently saw it) as a neutral background medium, rather than as a positive, active ingredient in productive processes. It is this philosophic perspective that underlies the pure time-preference theory to be discussed in this paper. Given this philosophic perspective, then, we note that the interest problem has, therefore, thus far not been touched in the slightest by any productivity-of-roundaboutness considerations.

The Pure Time-Preference Theory of Interest

The alternative "Austrian" theory of interest that we wish to clarify in this paper, the PTPT, is that pursued consistently by the American Frank Fetter and by Ludwig von Mises. This theory solves the interest problem by appeal to widespread (possibly universal) positive time preference. If, in fact, people do prefer (other aspects of the situation aside) to achieve their goals sooner rather than later, then the dilemma posed by the machine and its rentals, or by the tree and its fruit, dissolves. The price paid for a tree tends systematically to fall short of the sum of its annual fruit yields because, when the tree is bought, the yields are only prospective yields. One is simply not prepared to pay $100 today in order to command $100 worth of fruit in five or ten years time, no matter how ironclad the contract for the fruit delivery may be. The prospect of $100 available in the future has less attractive power than does the prospect of $100 available immediately. The PTPT argues that this solution of the interest problem is entirely sufficient to account for the interest phenomena we observe, in *all* their manifestations, in the simplest consumption loan context (in the pure-exchange economy), or in the most complex of financial-industrial situations. After all, production processes do take time, hence the present price of input services must, given positive time preference, systematically and repeatedly, fall short of the nominal value yielded in the future by their marginal productivity. A portion of currently emerging output must then regularly be retained each year by the capitalist who has, sometime in the past, advanced the sums needed to pay for the input services whose output is now emerging. This retained interest income is not caused by, or made possible by, the physical productivity of anything.

Such time-preference considerations are able, then, to account completely for the phenomenon of interest. They are able, entirely without any appeal to productivity of roundaboutness, to answer the question formulated in the interest problem. On the other hand, as we have seen, the productivity of roundaboutness offered no solution at all to that problem (for those not recognizing waiting or time as a productive agent). Hence, in the view of its protagonists, this "pure" time-preference theory[11] is entirely adequate for its objective; *no productivity considerations can possibly enter at all into the explanation offered for interest.*

It is the latter contention that many theorists, from Böhm-Bawerk's time down to our own, have found simply incredible. These critics of PTPT find it unbelievable that the claim can be made that the market phenomenon of interest is never, in any way, under any circumstances, to be attributed to the productivity of capital or of roundaboutness, waiting, or time. It will be instructive to examine a recurring theme pursued by these critics in expressing their incredulity.

Sheep, Rice, and Austrian Hocus-Pocus

These critics argue that simple hypothetical examples demonstrate that, at least under certain conditions, a positive rate of interest necessarily emerges, being strictly determined by physical productivity. These examples, the critics maintain, demonstrate that the old argument with which Böhm-Bawerk had demolished the simple productivity theories (viz., the argument

---

[11] See Ingo Pellengahr, "Austrians Versus Austrians I: A Subjectivist View of Interest," in *Studies in Austrian Capital Theory, Investment and Time*, M. Faber, ed. (Berlin, Heidelberg, and New York: Springer-Verlag, 1986), pp. 10–11, for several senses in which the adjective "pure" may be understood in the present context. Also, Pellengahr, "Austrians Versus Austrians II: Functionalist Versus Essentialist Theories of Interest," in *Studies in Austrian Capital Theory, Investment and Time*, M. Faber, ed. (Berlin, Heidelberg, and New York: Springer-Verlag, 1986).

that competition ought to drive the market price of the productive agent to the point where it no longer yields a value surplus) cannot entirely drive productivity considerations out of the interest-theoretic picture. Whether or not we can find a logical flaw in the Böhm-Bawerkian argument, the stylized "facts" of these examples prove the argument to be specious. Productivity considerations are clearly sufficient to account for interest. It cannot, therefore, be the case that the explanation of interest must run in *purely* time-preference terms. The examples used by these critics vary in their details. H.G. Brown talked of fruit trees,[12] Irving Fisher talked of sheep,[13] Knight talked of his Crusonia plant (an edible plant that grew at a fixed rate continuously),[14] quite recently Samuelson constructed a rice example to drive home an essentially similar point. What these examples have in common is (1) that they postulate a given rate of physical productivity to the capital stock, a rate invariant to scale of production or level of wealth; (2) that these examples *appear*, at least at first glance, to escape the impact of the traditional Böhm-Bawerkian argument (against productivity theories of interest) by confining the example to the context of a single good world (in which the critics believe value productivity measures must coincide with physical productivity rates).[15] Let us examine the most recent of these examples, Samuelson's rice case (which he raised in a discussion of a different doctrinal issue).

Samuelson's case was introduced in the course of a recent critical reconsideration of Schumpeter's zero-interest doctrine.[16]

---

12 H.G. Brown, "The Discount Versus the Cost-of-Production Theory of Capital Valuation," *American Economic Review* (June, 1914).
13 Irving Fisher, *The Theory of Interest* (New York: Macmillan, 1930), p. 193.
14 Frank H. Knight, "Diminishing Returns from Investment," *Journal of Political Economy* (March, 1944): 52.
15 Brown was dismayed at having been thought by Fetter to have failed to recognize the problem of value productivity. He believed himself to have successfully avoided this pitfall by his example. See H.G. Brown, *Economic Science and the Common Welfare*, 3rd ed. (Columbia, Mo.: Lucas Brothers, 1926), p. 125, n. 13.
16 Paul A. Samuelson, "Schumpeter as an Economic Theorist," in *Schumpeterian Economics*, H. Frisch, ed. (New York: Praeger, 1981).

Schumpeter had argued (on the basis of reasoning reflecting Böhm-Bawerk's arguments against the productivity theories of interest) that in a world in circular-flow equilibrium, the rate of interest must be zero, with all output value decomposed into land, rent, and labor wages, with nothing left for any interest share. Samuelson objects that a *possible* technological case refutes the Schumpeterian argument. The case Samuelson identifies is that of 100 units of rice ripening into 110 units of rice during the period of one year, without the input of any labor or any scarce land. This case shows, Samuelson claims, that final value need *not* necessarily be wholly swept back through the market as factor payments to labor and land; apparently we have 10 units of rice ("real interest income") that can be attributed to no factor service—only to the productivity through time of the initial rice stock. Mere ownership of rice capital confers title to a possible perpetual flow of annual rice consumption income. This annual income is clearly interest earned by the rice capitalist. This income is accounted for entirely by the physical productivity of rice. Samuelson hastens to anticipate the obvious Schumpeterian response. Schumpeter had emphasized that, with interest zero, "the greater magnitude of the forest is *already* imputed back in value to the saplings." So that today's 100 units of rice already have the value of next year's 110 units: "these foreseen changes ... only conserve the already calculated value of the process," without involving any creation of new value. But Samuelson hotly denounces this response as

> pure deception. Real rice *is* being produced net. Kuznets can measure it. You can eat 10 [units of] rice every year and still not impair your circular flow income.... No hocus-pocus of backward imputation—of forest to sapling, or rice grain to rice grain—evades the naive fact of productive interest.[17]

It may be instructive to note how this kind of example *appears* to escape the Böhm-Bawerkian critique. Naive productivity theories explain the interest on the capital sum invested in a tree

---

17 Samuelson, "Schumpeter as an Economic Theorist," p. 23.

by virtue of the tree's physical fecundity. Böhm-Bawerk's criticism pointed out that physical productivity does not necessarily mean value productivity. In value terms it is surely still possible, in principle, for the value of the tree to be equal to the sum of the values of all future fruit crops. The presently considered fruit tree, sheep, and rice examples *seem* to escape this problem. One writer has in fact claimed[18] that this is the outstanding virtue of the single-good economy (he is thinking specifically of Knight's Crusonia-plant economy). Rates of productivity can be arrived at directly, since "capital stock" and "income" consist of the same physical entities. No resort need be had to calculation in "value terms," with all its attendant pitfalls. So that these productivity examples, from sheep to Crusonia to rice, do indeed demonstrate that, even with zero rate of time preference, present rice exchanges for future rice at a rate that expresses the physical productivity of rice. If *this* demonstration were enough to settle the problem posed by the phenomenon of interest, the issue would indeed be closed. Time preference need have nothing to do with the emergence of interest; interest as a phenomenon, and the particular *rate* of interest established in the market *can*, it is clear, be entirely explained by physical productivity (at least in certain contexts). Yet the matter is far less simple than this.

Interest, Own-Rates of Interest, and Intertemporal Exchange

What these examples demonstrate is that physical productivity affects (or even "determines") the intertemporal exchange rate (the own-rate of interest) on sheep, on rice, and on Crusonia, respectively. One hundred units of 1987 rice exchange, in 1987, for 110 promised units of 1988 rice. With this trade repeated each year, the rice owner can consume 10 units of rice each year ("real interest income") without eroding the ("capital") base that

---

18 Donald Dewey, *Modern Capital Theory* (New York and London: Columbia University Press, 1965), p. 80.

yields this annual income. We shall attempt to show, however, that from the Fetter–Mises PTPT view, these demonstrations do nothing to advance understanding of the general phenomenon of interest; nor do they, as we shall see, demonstrate the impotence or irrelevancy of Böhm-Bawerk's refutation of simple productivity theories.

It may be useful to review the impasse we have apparently reached. On the one hand, these sheep and rice stories show that an annual consumption income drawn from the physical fecundity of a source can in principle be indefinitely enjoyed without eroding the continued existence and productiveness of that source. On the other hand, the *logic* of the Böhm-Bawerkian reasoning refuting productivity theories of interest has not itself been addressed—the reasoning has been denounced as hocus-pocus not because of any demonstrated logical fallacy but apparently because these sheep and rice cases are supposed to serve as counterexamples showing precisely that phenomenon which the Böhm-Bawerkian reasoning purported to have proven to be impossible.

Reflection should surely convince us: (*a*) that the Böhm-Bawerkian reasoning must still be reckoned with—after all, no flaw in its logic has as yet been identified in these examples; (*b*) that these examples demonstrate the possibility of an income *different* from that for which Böhm-Bawerk sought an explanation—the possibility, that is, of an income *which the Böhm-Bawerkian reasoning never questioned*; (*c*) that since it was the Böhm-Bawerkian reasoning that underlay what we have called the interest problem, *that* interest problem has *not* been touched at all by these sheep and rice stories. Let us try to explain all this. We must return to our original statement of the interest problem.

The interest problem, we recall, asked how it is possible for an individual to invest capital funds in a way that yields a perpetual net income. Why does not the market bid up the price of all the "machines" (in which the individual might plan to invest his capital) so that no net annual yield remains. This question, it should be noted, did not challenge the physical possibility of a tree of infinite life producing an annual crop of fruit (or a tree of finite life producing an annual crop of fruit large enough to permit the planting, out of fruit output, of a replacement tree when the parent tree dies). The question merely asked why, in the absence of any other theory of interest, the market does not bid up the price of the tree to the point where in fact no net annual financial yield is possible from investing in trees. This is what Fetter hammered away at, the distinction between goods and values in this context: "A theory of interest must be *essentially* a value-theory."[19] Samuelson has proven that ownership of rice permits an indefinite stream of annual rice consumption; he has not disproved the contention that the anticipated perpetual flow of rice consumption is already fully recorded in the market valuation of the initial rice source. Samuelson does not, in fact, appear to wish to deny this contention; he appears merely to conclude that this contention constitutes a meaningless incantation which does not affect the undeniable realities of perpetual annual consumption flows—duly measured by Kuznets, or somebody.

One can sympathize with Samuelson's impatience at verbal mysticism that seems out of touch with palpable reality. Moreover we can go a little further; Samuelson was dealing not with any theory of interest, but with Schumpeter's belief that—regardless of productivity—in the state of circular flow no interest at all would emerge. It is easy to sympathize with Samuelson's sense of conviction that his rice example has shown that productivity interest can indeed emerge in this state of affairs. Yet it must be pointed out that when we turn to a world somewhat richer in assumptions than Samuelson's rice model, it becomes clear that his example (and also the earlier fruit tree, sheep, and Crusonia stories) have in fact failed to identify interest income (in the sense in which we have identified the interest problem) as a productivity return.

---

19 Fetter, "Capitalization versus Productivity: Rejoinder," 257.

One hundred units of 1987 rice are expected to ripen into 110 units of 1988 rice. Suppose that the "value" of the 100 units of 1987 rice has indeed risen to anticipate this physical growth. Then in terms of the interest problem (formulated at the outset of this paper) the perpetual annual rice consumption income so made possible *does not present an example of interest*. The annual flow of rice income is indeed adequately explained by productivity—more to the point, there was no "problem" that demanded explanation, at all. There is, after all, no problem constituted by the circumstance that a tree yields fruit annually.

The interest problem would begin, in the context of the rice example, only if in fact the "value" of the 100 units of 1987 rice is somehow lower than that of 110 units of 1988 rice. *Then* we would have the possibility of a sum of abstract capital value serving as a financial source somehow generating a flow of *greater* subsequent value. *That* would indeed appear to fly in the face of economic intuition (since competition ought—absent a theory of interest—to be expected to exclude such a phenomenon). And it is of course *this* interest problem that PTPT solves by reference to the general subjective preference for the achievement of goals sooner rather than later.

What the preceding asserts, then, is that what Brown, Fisher, Knight, and Samuelson have identified as interest income—and which they apparently view as the *only* interest income needed to be discussed—is *in fact not interest income at all* (from the perspective of the interest problem formulated above). On the other hand, that interest income which PTPT deals with—an income which *does* fit the specifications of interest as formulated above—turns out to be something the very existence of which the critics appear to deny. (We recall that Schumpeter, too, was [in this respect only!] on the side of the critics of PTPT: he believed that in the circular-flow no pure interest would be present.) Obviously the entire debate appears to have degenerated into a squabble about the meaning of terms.

From the Fisherian perspective the semantic bickering may appear even more deplorable. After all, the Fisherian view is that interest, the income received in return for providing services of "waiting," is *at the same time*, the reward received by the capitalists (who provide these services) for their sacrifices (sacrifices which obtain their poignancy from the prevalence of positive time preferences). A discussion such as the above (in which the issue is made to appear whether the term interest income is to refer to the fruits of rice fecundity or to a value differential attributed to time preference) must seem doubly regrettable. Let us go back to basics.

The Interest Problem that Calls For Solution: The Competing Versions

The attention of economists over the centuries has been attracted to the real-world, palpable, phenomenon of interest income largely due to its "surplus" character. Apparently it is possible, in the market economy, to command a steady, regular income merely by possession of a capital stock. As Böhm-Bawerk introduced the phenomenon:

> Whoever is the owner of a capital sum is ordinarily able to derive from it a permanent net income.... This income ... arises independently of any personal act of the capitalist. It accrues to him even though he has not moved a finger in creating it.... It can be derived from any capital, no matter what be the kind of goods of which the capital consists, from naturally fruitful, as well as from barren goods, from perishable as well as from durable goods, from replaceable as well as from irreplaceable goods, from money as well as from commodities. And, finally, it flows without ever exhausting the capital from which it arises, and therefore without any necessary limit to its continuance.... And so the phenomenon of interest presents, on the whole, the remarkable picture of a lifeless thing, capital, producing an everlasting and inexhaustible supply of goods.[20]

With this starting point for discussions of the interest phenomenon, it is easy to see how physical fecundity (while it offers

---

20 Böhm-Bawerk, *Capital and Interest*, p. 1.

a tempting ingredient for interest theorizing) came to be dismissed (in Böhm-Bawerk's chapter refuting the productivity theories). The point is that the entire discussion begins with the assertion that *value* productivity is a common fact of life; this fact of life was, after all, asserted to hold for barren goods and for money just as it holds for naturally fruitful goods and for commodities. It was this Böhm-Bawerkian identification of the problem as referring to value productivity that was at the heart of the formulation of the interest problem cited at the start of this paper. Now, the prospective interest theorist can choose one or the other of only two options: he can deny that this interest phenomenon in fact exists (so that there is nothing to be explained), or he must seek an explanation for it within its own framework. Schumpeter chose the first option. Others, implicitly denying the phenomenon that Böhm-Bawerk took as his starting point, focus on physical productivity as a sufficient basis for the (undeniable) *market* phenomenon of interest. But in so doing they have not offered a new explanation for the Böhm-Bawerkian phenomenon: they have simply denied its existence, and chosen instead to talk about something else—something easily confused with it (because both might serve plausibly as underlying basis for the *surface* phenomenon of market interest). PTPT theorists are then entitled to accept the existence of the Böhm-Bawerkian phenomenon and to offer their own explanation for it. From this perspective, then, the situation can be summed up as follows:

First, there is a commonly observed phenomenon of market interest. No one disputes this observation. Second, for Böhm-Bawerk this phenomenon of market interest is simply the expression of the existence of an underlying phenomenon of pure value productivity. This interpretation of market interest renders the phenomenon insoluble through reference to physical productivity, and leaves it calling out for alternative explanation. Third, PTPT accepts this Böhm-Bawerkian interpretation (and offered time-preference insights to account for the phenomenon of value productivity). Fourth, Schumpeter, while not disputing the

Böhm-Bawerkian interpretation of the observed phenomenon of market interest, held that this entire phenomenon is a transient one that would disappear in the state of circular flow. Fifth, other theorists dispute Böhm-Bawerk's interpretation of the observed phenomenon of market interest. In effect these writers deny the existence of the (underlying "value productivity") phenomenon which Böhm-Bawerk asserted to be reflected in the observed phenomenon of market interest. For these writers the observed phenomenon of market interest reflects nothing more than physical productivity; there *is* no "value productivity" to be explained. Sixth, finally, for modern theorists following Fisher, the entire discussion in the present section represents an incomprehensible lapse into meaningless mysticism and metaphysics. For these theorists the task of a theory of interest is *not at all that of solving the problem formulated at the start of this paper* (and expressive of the Böhm-Bawerkian formulation at the start of this section). Were the Fisherians to consider *that* (Böhm-Bawerkian) question, they would consider it solved immediately once one has identified "waiting" as a missing factor. Since waiting is a scarce, costly factor, its market value tends to equal *both* its marginal product *and* its marginal cost (in terms of foregone sooner consumption). Interest is *both* the reward for sacrificed earlier consumption *and* the fruits of the enhanced output made possible by waiting. For Fisher and the modern writers the interesting question, and thus the task of interest theory is (quite apart from possible disputes concerning the existence of the phenomenon to which the Böhm-Bawerkian formulation refers) *nothing more than that of identifying the determinants of intertemporal prices.* In undertaking this latter task, Fisher develops a perfectly adequate framework in which *both* physical productivity *and* time-preference considerations have their place.

We may conclude then: (*a*) Most of the modern bewilderment of PTPT stems, we would argue, from the Fisherian unconcern with the interest problem that was posed by Böhm-Bawerk. Most moderns, following Fisher, do not see the task of interest theory to be to account for a phenomenon that somehow (in the absence of a theory of interest) "ought not to exist." As a result, the Fisherian approach finds the PTPT view bizarre (since their own approach finds time preference and physical productivity *both* valuable elements in their theory). We shall return to consider this Fisherian view of PTPT in the subsequent section. (*b*) Sheep, rice, and other stories introduced to demonstrate the adequacy of a pure productivity theory (and thus to refute PTPT) express a different misunderstanding of PTPT. Without recognizing it, the authors of these examples have in effect denied the very existence of the phenomenon which Böhm-Bawerk identified as that calling for explanation (i.e., the underlying phenomenon of pure value productivity). From the Böhm-Bawerkian point of view, therefore, these stylized examples deal with a phenomenon which (1) is other than the one Böhm-Bawerk is concerned with, and (2) offers no theoretical challenges ("of course" trees produce fruit!).

We have thus identified *two* distinct sources of modern bewilderment with PTPT. One source stems from an implicit denial of the value-productivity phenomenon seen as calling for explanation in Böhm-Bawerk's view (and in PTPT's view). From this denial it was easy to move to assuming that the phenomenon to be explained by a theory of interest is that which would underlie the market rate of interest *in the absence of* the value-productivity phenomenon—viz., physical productivity. From this latter perspective, PTPT's refusal to accord to physical productivity any role appears simply incomprehensible. The *second* source of modern bewilderment stems, not from any denial of the phenomenon that Böhm-Bawerk sought to explain, but from an entirely different conception of what constitutes the function of a theory of interest. Whereas for Böhm-Bawerk a theory of interest is called for to account for an otherwise inexplicable phenomenon, for Fisher a theory of interest is called for to identify the determinants of a particular market rate of exchange (viz., the intertemporal rate, which implicitly expresses the rate of interest). From this Fisherian perspective it is easy to understand how bizarre it appears for anyone to deny any role for physical productivity in a theory of interest. We turn to elaborate on this last point. The point turns out to involve an old dispute between Fisher and Böhm-Bawerk that throws considerable light on the entire issue.

The Existence of Interest vs. the Rate of Interest

"Some writers," Fisher wrote, "have chosen, for purposes of exposition, to postulate two questions involved in the theory of the rate of interest, viz., (1) why any rate of interest exists and (2) how the rate of interest is determined."[21] Fisher dismisses this distinction as being unilluminating, "since to explain how the rate of interest is determined involves the question of whether the rate can or cannot be zero."[22] The purpose of the present section of this paper is (a) to present the case for the distinction criticized by Fisher—a distinction in fact made by Böhm-Bawerk, as we shall see—and (b) to show how failure to understand the rationale for the distinction has generated the widespread modern bewilderment with PTPT referred to earlier.

No better defense for Böhm-Bawerk's distinction need be found than the lucid discussion that he himself provided. Böhm-Bawerk was criticizing Fisher for not distinguishing between "originating forces" and "determining forces":

> All interest-originating causes undoubtedly are also determining factors for the actual rate. But not all rate-determining factors are also interest-creating causes.... When we inquire into the causes of a flood we certainly cannot cite the dams and reservoirs built to prevent or at least mitigate inundations. But they are a determining factor for the actual watermark of the flood.... Similarly, there are other circumstances besides the actual interest-creating causes that bring about

---

21 Fisher, *The Theory of Interest*, pp. 13f. and 474 (where Böhm-Bawerk is identified, without specific citation, as having argued for this distinction).
22 Ibid. See also J.W. Conard, *An Introduction to the Theory of Interest* (Berkeley and Los Angeles: University of California Press, 1959), pp. 13–14.

or enhance the value advantage of present goods over future goods.[23]

It will be observed that Böhm-Bawerk's distinction faithfully expresses the formulation of the interest problem that he offered (as cited in the preceding section). There is a phenomenon (the existence of interest income) which calls for explanation (just as the occurrence of floods calls for explanation). The required explanation need not necessarily invoke all those "forces" which may be relevant for the determination of the particular rate of interest prevailing in the market. It is true that a complete listing of all aspects of all the "rate-determining forces" would at the same time explain why the interest rate is other than zero. But to say that all these forces are responsible for the interest phenomenon would be highly misleading. If someone stands amazed at the flow of city traffic along one of its central avenues during morning rush hour, and asks, "Why is traffic so heavy?", the answer to the question should presumably run in terms of the need of people to get to work. It will simply not do to invoke the traffic-light system as an explanation (even partially) for the volume of traffic (even though it is certainly the case that the size of that volume has been, in part, determined by that traffic-light system). For Fisher, it is quite clear, the "problem" of interest is simply to provide a full catalogue of the rate-determining forces. Fisher's analysis leads him, inevitably, to recognize the interaction, among these forces, of physical productivity and time preference. Modern theorists, following Fisher, are understandably bewildered by PTPT statements denying any role for physical productivity. But to endorse the PTPT denial of a role for physical productivity is not necessarily to deny that physical productivity is to be listed among the forces combining to determine intertemporal rates of exchange. The PTPT's denial refers strictly to the problem of accounting for the phenomenon of interest. For the solution of *this* problem, PTPT finds physical productivity

---

23 Böhm-Bawerk, *Capital and Interest*, p. 192.

to be no more relevant than traffic lights are (for accounting for the phenomenon of morning rush hour traffic) or than dams are (for Böhm-Bawerk's example of accounting for the occurrence of floods).

PTPT exponents often drive home the irrelevance of physical productivity by pointing out that physical productivity is neither necessary nor sufficient for an explanation for interest (in the sense of value productivity).[24] They point out how, in the absence of time preference, physical productivity, no matter how great, cannot generate value productivity. And they point out how, even in a pure exchange world without production processes of any kind, the phenomenon of value productivity could arise as a result of time-preference considerations exclusively. One critic responded to this reasoning by asking whether, based on parallel reasoning, one would conclude that the striking of matches is irrelevant to the causation of fire (since not every match that is struck produces fire, and not all matches that ignite do so as a result of having been struck). The response should surely be that the striking of matches is certainly *highly* relevant to the prevalence of match ignition, but the striking of matches is indeed far less relevant for other questions, such as, e.g., why ignition occurs among matches rather than among Q-tips.

Admittedly, some expositions of PTPT have sometimes unfortunately permitted it to be thought that, since only time preference accounts for the *existence* of interest, it follows that a change in the conditions of physical productivity would invariably leave the rate of interest unchanged. But in fact PTPT implies nothing of the kind.[25] It is one thing to maintain that normal daily nutritional needs are in no way responsible for the existence of hospitals; it in no way follows that the extent of such needs is not a factor helping determine the size (and conceivably even

---

24 Charles W. Baird, *Prices and Markets, Intermediate Microeconomics*, 2nd ed. (St. Paul, Minn.: West Publishing, 1982), pp. 303f.
25 Fetter was quite explicit on this point, see "Capitalization versus Productivity: Rejoinder," 247.

the number) of hospitals. *Given* the presence of sickness (upon which the existence of hospitals does depend), a host of unrelated matters may participate in the determination of hospital size. Similarly PTPT theorists do recognize that since the prevalence of positive time preference does generate the phenomenon of interest, it cannot at all be ruled out that other factors (including physical productivity) may affect the determination of its rate. For example, physical productivity may significantly affect the level of wealth, and thus the marginal rate of time preference. All PTPT insists on is that, no matter how significant a role physical productivity may play among the complete list of variables affecting the rate of interest, it is fallacious to refer to interest income (expressing value productivity) as the fruit of the physical productivity of agents of production. No matter how heavily the costs of the hospital meal service weigh in the determination of hospital size, it remains a fallacy to see a hospital as a sleep-in restaurant.[26]

Some Remarks on Methodological Essentialism

It will be observed that our defense of PTPT against the bewilderment evinced by its various critics, amounts to a partial affirmation of what has sometimes been termed "methodological essentialism." Several historians of thought have noticed that

---

[26] Economists have frequently argued (e.g., F.A. Hayek, "Time Preference and Productivity: A Reconsideration," *Economica*, n.s., 12 [1945]: 22–25) that whether time preference or physical productivity is to be considered the more important explanatory variable for interest, depends on which of them is expressed, in the standard Fisher diagram, by a curve having greater convexity. This makes good sense in regard to the determinants of the interest *rate*. It may be highly relevant to know whether the interest rate is more sensitive to a given marginal change in time preferences, than to a similar marginal change in physical productivity. But for the explanation of the *existence* of interest, these comparisons are hardly relevant. Even if hospital size were somehow more sensitive to changing nutritional standards than to change in the incidence of disease, the *raison d'etre* of the hospital remains unaffected.

for Menger, economic science is a search for *the reality underlying economic phenomena*—for their *essence (das Wesen)*. In a letter to Walras, Menger asks, "How can we attain to a knowledge of this essence, for example, the essence of value, the essence of land rent, the essence of entrepreneur's profit ... by mathematics?"[27] This search for essences, reflecting a philosophical approach attributed to Aristotelian influence,[28] would focus, then, not on the land rent paid for a particular parcel of real estate in a particular year, but upon those essential features of land rent that would be common to all examples of the phenomenon. Similarly an essentialist approach to the interest problem as posed by Böhm-Bawerk would focus not on the list of elements which together determine specific interest rates, but on those elements upon which the interest phenomenon essentially depends, elements without which the phenomenon could in fact not exist. PTPT finds these essential elements for the interest phenomenon in time preference. Physical productivity is *not* such an essential element of interest; but, to repeat, to affirm all this is not to deny that market rates of interest may be related to physical productivity conditions. To assert that, absent time preference, physical productivity is unable to generate *any* interest (in the sense of value productivity) is not to assert that, *given* time preference, the intertemporal rate of exchange, even in the form of the rate of value productivity, is unaffected by changes in the physical productivity of machines or of trees. All that is being asserted is that whatever role is played by physical productivity does not permit us to say that interest (value productivity) *is* the fruit of productive capital. (Rush hour traffic as a phenomenon may indeed be vitally affected by the timing of traffic lights; nonetheless we understand why it is accurate to describe the phenomenon of

---

[27] This letter is cited in Terence W. Hutchison, *A Review of Economic Doctrines, 1870–1929* (Oxford: Clarendon Press, 1953), p. 148.
[28] See Emil Kauder, *A History of Marginal Utility Theory* (Princeton, N.J.: Princeton University Press, 1965), p. 97; Samuel Bostaph, "The Methodological Debate Between Carl Menger and the German Historicists," *Atlantic Economic Journal* (September, 1978): 11.

rush hour traffic as "people getting to work," rather than as "the result of traffic-light timing.")

From the perspective of a modernist impatient with metaphysical discussion, some of this defense of PTPT against modernist "bewilderment" may appear wholly unhelpful; in fact it may confirm the critic's impression that it is all empty philosophizing unrelated to objective phenomena. If one sees the objective of science as being to account for empirical reality, and one sees the objective of price theory to explain the structure and levels of particular prices, then it will seem only natural to seek for an interest theory that explains particular rates of interest. All else must appear metaphysical, irrelevant, and plain confusing. So long as our theory of interest, say, in the form of Fisher's standard diagram (incorporating both intertemporal productive possibilities and time preferences), can show how the market in fact generates its intertemporal rates of exchange (with respect to given physically defined commodities identified at different dates), surely our scientific task has been accomplished—without any essentialist pursuit of some metaphysical reality underlying the explained phenomena. But this modernist impatience can be shown to be unreasonable. Such a demonstration requires that we recognize the nature of the delicate interface between science and ideology. It will prove convenient to present our discussion in the context of brief reference to the celebrated Cambridge Capital Controversy of recent decades.

Science and Ideology: The Cambridge Controversy and PTPT

For present purposes, we compress our account of the Cambridge Controversy to its barest relevant elements. One side of the debate, representing neoclassical orthodoxy, sees the phenomena of the capitalist economy, especially the assignment of income shares (including interest income), as being phenomena to be understood within the framework of market equilibrium. Market prices (and thus interest) have to be paid if consumers are to receive that which the productive capacity of the market is able to provide, and for which the consumers are prepared to pay. Interest is rendered necessary and thus, in a sense, "justified" by efficiency (i.e., consumer sovereignty) considerations.

On the other hand, the critics in Cambridge (England) vigorously deny that interest incomes are "caused by individual exchanges as constrained by technology and the availability of factors of production."[29] These critics see the distribution of income between wage earners and interest receivers as being determined by such considerations as the power balance between workers and capitalists, rather than by marginal products, consumer preferences, and factor supplies.

It is not difficult to recognize the ideological implications that can be drawn from each of these two views. As Robert Solow (representing the neoclassical side of the debate) observed, the Cambridge School saw neoclassical theory as "an important part of an apology for private capitalism. It sounds as if capitalists are entitled to their profits."[30] Indeed, Joan Robinson, leading figure in the Cambridge School, asserted very explicitly: "The unconscious preoccupation behind the neoclassical system was chiefly to raise profits to the same level of moral respectability as wages."[31] Clearly the Cambridge critics believe that their own theory of capital provides no such comfort and solace for the capitalist system.

It may be submitted that these asserted ideological implications of alternative capital theories are profoundly important for one's appreciation of what economic science can reveal. While Solow and others[32] believe the Cambridge attack on neoclassicism expresses an anti-capitalist animus, they do not deny the

---

29 See Hausman, *Capital, Profits and Prices*, p. 167.
30 Robert Solow, "Cambridge and the Real World," *Times Literary Supplement* (March 14, 1975).
31 Joan Robinson, *Economic Philosophy* (Chicago: Aldine, 1962), p. 58.
32 Mark Blaug, *The Cambridge Revolution: Success or Failure? A Critical Analysis of Cambridge Theories of Value and Distribution* (London: Institute of Economic Affairs, 1974).

responsibility to deal dispassionately with the Cambridge substantive criticisms and theory. Nor do the Cambridge critics fail to recognize that any ideological dissatisfaction with the implications of neoclassicism must yield to a dispassionate search for logical flaws in that theory. The important point is that such dispassionate scientific debate holds the key to the normative, non-scientific characterization of specific income categories. The neoclassical view of interest permits it to be seen as a productivity return (parallel to the way in which market wages are perceived). This is seen to permit the view that interest is on the "same level of moral respectability as wages." The Cambridge theory is one from which such innate respectability for interest income does *not* emerge. We wish to argue briefly here that the Cambridge Capital Controversy offered an array of alternative theoretical positions that was not exhaustive. A third point of view, not represented in the discussion, but one highly relevant to the underlying ideological concerns, is in fact to be found in the PTPT.

The neoclassical side of the debate saw interest as a productivity return. Any ideological defense of capitalist interest based on this side of the debate will consist in "justifying" interest as the proceeds of enhanced productivity made possible by scarce, costly waiting. In denying this defense, the Cambridge position will argue that interest is *not* the "justified" proceeds of productivity. (Rather it is a share of "social surplus" somehow acquired by owners of capital.) What needs now to be pointed out is that PTPT offers an understanding of interest income that may be seen as supporting its moral "respectability," but *without* seeing it as the fruits of productivity. From the PTPT perspective, the neoclassically implied defense of capitalism is flawed. We have again and again pointed out how PTPT does not recognize market interest income as constituting a productivity return; that is not what interest income *is*. On the other hand, PTPT very definitely sees market interest as expressing a market-determined rate of intertemporal exchange. So that PTPT provides a basis, if one chooses to use it for such a purpose, for a justification of interest (as a legitimate expression of consumer preferences) that nonetheless agrees with Cambridge critics that interest is not a productivity return.

The point of all this is that we cannot, surely, close our eyes to possible ideological implications of science. Our science may well be, perhaps, ideologically untainted and value free (or, at any rate, honest efforts in this direction may be undertaken), but human beings are, as valuing citizens, vitally interested in the character of controversial phenomena. If one is asked, "What justifies interest?", it will simply not do to defend it as reward for productivity, if analysis shows that that is not what it *is*. Note that for ideological (i.e., for normative, evaluative) purposes, methodological essentialism is highly relevant. One can hardly arrive at a judgment concerning the defensibility of interest income by showing that its size depends upon physical productivity. A "theory of hospitals" that fails to identify hospitals in terms of the essentiality of their medical character is likely to be less than helpful for the purposes of normative evaluation by citizens. Citizens asked to vote to support hospitals seen as sleep-in restaurants may respond differently than when hospitals are correctly seen as institutions fighting to contain dread diseases. There is every reason for science to take note of the non-scientific purposes for which scientific results may be helpfully consulted. From this perspective, the methodologically essentialist aspects of PTPT may be considered valuable features of it, rather than as obfuscating metaphysics.

Conclusion

Our defense of PTPT against modern "bewilderment" has dealt primarily with its apparently astounding assertion that physical productivity has *nothing* essentially to do with the phenomenon of interest. Our discussion has: (1) made it clear that PTPT does not necessarily deny a role for physical productivity in interest rate determination; (2) emphasized that what PTPT addresses is a question that is *different* from that of interest rate determination;

(3) identified the problem dealt with by PTPT as the interest problem addressed by Böhm-Bawerk, viz., what accounts for the phenomenon of net value-productivity (in the face of market competition that might be expected to squeeze it out of existence); (4) shown that PTPT's refusal to recognize any physical productivity role in the explanation for the existence of interest income rests on (the admittedly arbitrary) view that time and waiting are not to be seen as productive agents; (5) recognized the methodologically essentialist aspects of PTPT and argued for their relevance, especially in the context of the Cambridge Capital Controversy, for citizens' normative understanding of interest income; (6) made it clear how numerous stylized examples (sheep, rice, Crusonia, etc.) designed to demonstrate the essential role played by physical productivity in interest income generation, in fact, concern a phenomenon quite different from that upon which the Böhm-Bawerkian discussion focused. Regardless of one's opinion of the significance of income generated by physical productivity, we have emphasized the legitimacy of distinguishing between that income and the quite different income concept identified by Böhm-Bawerk and addressed by PTPT.

The upshot of the discussion, then, is that PTPT affirms the phenomenon of pure value-productivity, that is, the phenomenon in which a source of value at a given date generates a flow of values during subsequent periods that exceeds, in total, the value of the source. PTPT accounts for this phenomenon by reference to widespread (possibly universal) preference for the earlier, rather than later, achievement of goals. Market rates of interest, and market interest income, are expressions of this underlying phenomenon of value productivity (and of its PTPT roots).

Interest Theories, Old and New

{ By Frank A. Fetter }

Abstract theory, always of fundamental importance, has, as truly as practical policy, its "topics of the day," and just now discussion of the interest problem is especially active. Notable among recent articles are those by Professors H.R. Seager, Irving Fisher, and H.G. Brown.[1] Mere individual differences of opinion concern us little; but certain impersonal equities which other students of economics have in the interest problem, are involved; for in recent discussion is fairly presented the issue between the old and the new conception of the interest problem.[2] And yet the case for the newer view might seem to be on the point of being

---

Reprinted from *American Economic Review* 4, no. 1 (March 1914).

[1] H.R. Seager, (critique) "The Impatience Theory of Interest," *American Economic Review* 2, no. 4 (December, 1912): 834–51; Irving Fisher, (reply) "The Impatience Theory of Interest," *American Economic Review* 3, no. 3 (September, 1913): 610–18; H.R. Seager, (comment) "The Impatience Theory of Interest," *American Economic Review* 3, no. 3 (September, 1913): 618–19; Harry G. Brown, "The Marginal Productivity versus the Impatience Theory of Interest," *Quarterly Journal of Economics* 27, no. 4 (August, 1913): 630–50.

[2] To prevent misunderstanding, let us say that Böhm-Bawerk is here classed among those holding to the old theory, for his "roundabout process" explanation is technological, though united with strong psychological features in the explanation of consumption loans.

lost before the bar of economic opinion. It is a duty, therefore, to attempt a more adequate statement of the neglected truths.

The rival views may be characterized as the technological[3] and the psychological interest theories. For more than a decade, the psychological theory has been gaining adherents in America. There has not been lacking adverse criticism in scattered book reviews and in occasional footnotes; but in the main, the opposition has been of a merely negative sort, in that most economists have failed to reckon with it and have adhered to the older theory.

Professor Irving Fisher as a Productivity Theorist

Seager's paper, just cited, is the first systematic attempt that has been made to disprove any version of the newer theory (for Fisher's "impatience theory," which Seager attacks, has been generally supposed to be a psychological theory). The discussion started by Seager necessarily follows in large part the lines determined by Fisher's treatment. Let us first, therefore, try to get our bearings as to that. My own position on the general question involved in this discussion has in the past been with Fisher so far and so long as he adhered to a psychological explanation. And yet, I must recognize the merit of Seager's argument in several respects, and, as a psychological theorist, I find myself more disquieted by Fisher's reply than by Seager's direct attack. Particularly regrettable is the impression of confession and avoidance which Fisher gives. He seems to capitulate on the main issue. To the charge that he failed "to take account of the elements of productivity or the technique of production," Fisher enters a denial[4] in terms which seem to imply that he is a good productivity theorist. This reply comes as a surprise even to those who were aware of certain ambiguous expressions on this point in

---

3 This somewhat unusual word is here employed in the sense of physically productive, a technological interest theory being one which finds the explanation of the rate of interest in the actual, practical performances, or uses, of agents in producing other goods.

4 Fisher, (reply) "Impatience Theory of Interest," 610.

Fisher's writings. For if he has not meant to deny, in his previous writings, the validity of productivity theories, one knows not what to believe. Here are some significant passages:

> There are many who, consciously or unconsciously, ascribe the phenomena of interest to the productivity of capital in general.... Yet a very slight examination will suffice to show the inadequacy of this explanation.[5]
>
> To raise the rate of interest by raising the productivity of capital is, therefore, like trying to raise oneself by one's bootstraps.[6]
>
> Absence of interest is quite compatible with the presence of physical-productivity, and ... therefore whatever element is responsible for the existence of interest in the actual world, that element cannot be physical-productivity.[7]
>
> The conclusion, therefore, from our study of the various forms of the productivity theory is that physical-productivity, of itself, has no such direct relation to the rate of interest as is usually ascribed to it; and in the theories which we have examined, the rate of interest is always surreptitiously introduced.[8]
>
> "Interest is due to the productivity of capital." ... This proposition looks attractive, but it is superficial ... the superior productiveness of roundabout processes of production ... has no power whatever to create interest.[9]

Now, however, instead of meeting the question directly, and reaffirming his disbelief in the productivity theory, he seems to surrender his position as the easiest way of ridding himself of criticism. He says that he pleads "not guilty to the charge of neglecting the 'productivity' or 'technique' element." He speaks of "the true way in which the 'technique of production' enters into the determination of the rate of interest";[10]

---

[5] Irving Fisher, *The Rate of Interest: Its Nature, Determination, and Relation to Economic Phenomena* (New York: Macmillan, 1907), p. 12.
[6] Ibid., p. 15.
[7] Ibid., p. 22.
[8] Ibid., p. 28.
[9] Irving Fisher, "Impatience Theory of Interest," *Scientia* 9 (1911): 383, 384, 386.
[10] Fisher, (reply) "Impatience Theory of Interest," 610.

he says, "'the productivity' or 'technique' element, so far from being lacking in my theory, is one of its cardinal features";[11] and, again, "Productivity has not been neglected in my treatment of interest."

Now it is true that these somewhat general expressions alone merely raise the reader's doubts. For to say that he does not neglect "productivity" or that it is not lacking in his theory does not positively commit Fisher to belief in a productivity explanation of interest as distinct from an essentially psychological explanation. But other expressions deepen the reader's doubts, and suggest strongly that Fisher objects only to certain formulations of a productivity theory, not to productivity theories on principle.

He admits[12] that in his book he has criticized "*the ordinary*[13] productivity theories," but says that he then "explained to the reader that later in the book *I would rebuild the 'technical' feature* which, in the theories of others, I sought to destroy." Again[14] he speaks of his strictures on "*the ordinary* productivity theories," implying that some productivity theory or theories may be tenable. Again he reproaches Professor Seager with being "open to the charge of regarding all productivity theories as alike sound in principle" (implying that some *are* sound?). And he expresses the belief that "everyone who has read Böhm-Bawerk should believe that *the ordinary*, or as Böhm-Bawerk calls them, *the 'naive'* productivity theories are snares and delusions."[15]

These passages taken by themselves give the impression that the author is at heart as good a productivity theorist as anyone; indeed, he collates them himself, seemingly, for the purpose of producing just this impression. This clearly is out of accord with the spirit and letter of much else that Fisher has said in denying productivity as a causal explanation of interest. The most lenient

---

11 Fisher, (reply) "Impatience Theory of Interest," 610.
12 Ibid., 611.
13 My italics throughout.
14 Ibid.
15 Ibid., 617.

interpretation is that Fisher is here speaking in the spirit of an earlier statement:

> If after all has been said and understood, any one still prefers to call such a loan "productive," no objection is offered, provided always that it is made wholly clear what is meant by the term "productive."[16]

Here it seems clear that Fisher did not think the term productive, which he carefully enclosed in quotation marks each time, was a fitting adjective for such loans, made by borrowers for the purpose of gaining a profit. In his reply to Seager, however, Fisher's mood is all for so emphasizing any earlier statement of the tolerant sort as to make it appear that he does not deny the productivity theory of interest. He cites several passages in his earlier writings in which he has used such expressions as "the elements of truth contained in the claims of the productivity theories."[17] He says: "It was through mathematics that I saw the nature and importance of productivity in relation to interest," giving the impression that he at one time disbelieved in productivity as a causal explanation but had come to see his mistake. He says that his book "was written expressly for that purpose [rendering of the technique element]."[18] Despite his ability to adduce these evidences of his innocence of the charge of disbelief in the productivity interest theory, Fisher is penitent for not having made his position clearer. He declares that he has himself "to blame … for the mistakes he [Seager] has made." He concludes this recantation:

> I ought, I doubt not, to have put forward the productivity element more prominently and with less avoidance of the term "productivity." I remember consciously avoiding this term so far as possible lest the reader should associate my theory too much with *the many false theories of productivity*.[19]

---

16 Fisher, *Rate of Interest*, p. 251.
17 Fisher, (reply) "Impatience Theory of Interest," 612.
18 Ibid., 613.
19 Ibid., 617; my italics.

The most clear-cut evidence that he cites from his writings to prove that he never intended to deny the validity of the productivity theory per se is this: "Again I specifically stated (*Rate of Interest*, p. 186): 'But while the slowness of Nature is a sufficient cause for interest, her productivity is an additional cause.'"[20] A phrase which might have been deemed an oversight when taken in connection with other earlier statements is here deliberately reaffirmed, and casts doubt upon the meaning of much of Fisher's previous writings. Just what is his position on the productivity theory? His recent apology, appearing at the same time that his colleague, Dr. H.G. Brown, publishes an elaborate defense of an eclectic productivity theory, is most disappointing to the group of true psychological interest theorists in America, who a few years ago welcomed Professor Fisher as an accession to their ranks, and who still cherish the hope that, after he has fed for a time on the husks of the productivity theory, they may greet him again as a returning prodigal.

Origin of the Capitalization Theory

As a basis for further discussion, a brief review must be given of the origin and main features of "the capitalization theory" of interest as I had developed it several years before the publication of Professor Fisher's theory of interest in 1907. My attention was drawn to the subject repeatedly between the years 1895 and 1900 while I was studying the theory of distribution, and in an article on the capital concept, in 1900, I said:

> I would not exaggerate the significance of the change here proposed in the capital concept, yet it would be folly to ignore the consequences its acceptance would involve for economic theory.... The current theories of land value, of rent, of interest, to a greater or less extent rest on the unsound ideas which have been criticised throughout this paper. On another occasion the writer will attempt to state the outlines of an

---

20 Fisher, (reply) "Impatience Theory of Interest," 612.

economic system of thought in harmony with the capital concept here presented.[21]

Again, in a paper presented the same year at a meeting of the American Economic Association, it was said among other statements pointing in the same direction:

> With this change [of the capital concept] must go a change in the whole conception of interest, which likewise is connected in the still current treatment with a factor that has been produced by labor. The multitudinous and naive inconsistencies of the older treatment became apparent when viewed in the light of the later value theory.
>
> The doctrines of rent and interest as currently taught are hopelessly entangled in these old and illogical distinctions. The two forms of return for material goods must be considered as differing in modes of calculation, not as to kinds of agents and as kinds of return. The object of this paper may now be restated ... to show the necessity of rewriting the theory of distribution along radically new lines ... and the acceptance of doctrines, the readjustment of which is shown to be inevitable.[22]

More than a year later, in reviewing some essays by Böhm-Bawerk, I said:

> Great as have been the services of our author in stimulating to clearer and deeper thinking in economic theory, his presentation of a *Capitalstheorie* evidently is not destined to be a finality. Some development it is sure to undergo, and is undergoing. And that development lies along the lines of a value concept as opposed to a cost-of-production concept.[23]

---

21 Fetter, "Recent Discussion of the Capital Concept," *Quarterly Journal of Economics* 15, no. 1 (November, 1900): 45.
22 Frank Fetter, "The Next Decade of Economic Theory," *Publications of the American Economic Association*, 3rd series, 2, no. 1 (February, 1901): 240, 246; Papers and Proceedings of the Thirteenth Annual Meeting (December, 1900).
23 Frank Fetter, review of Eugen von Böhm-Bawerk's "Einige Strittige Fragen der Capitalstheorie," *Political Science Quarterly* 17 (March, 1902): 173.

Again in the same year, at the conclusion of a critical article on Böhm-Bawerk's theory:

> Let us venture an opinion as to the nature of the difficulty and the direction that must be taken to reach a correct solution.... Let us suggest the view that rent and interest are very dissimilar aspects of the value of goods. Rent[24] has to do with "production" of scarce and desirable uses of things. To the interest theorist this is in the nature, one might almost say, of an ultimate fact. The interest theory begins with the valuation of these different rents or incomes, distributed through different periods of time. The "productiveness" of a material agent is merely its quality of giving a scarce and desirable service to men. To explain this service of goods is the essence of the theory of rent. Given this and a prospective series of future services, however, the problem of interest arises, which is essentially that of explaining the valuation set on the future uses contained in goods. Interest thus expressing the exchange ratio of present and future services or uses is not and cannot be confined to any class of goods; it exists wherever there is a future service. It is not dependent on the roundaboutness of the process; for it exists where there is no process whatever, if there be merely a postponement of the use for the briefest period. A good interest theory must develop the fertile suggestion of Böhm-Bawerk that the interest problem is not one of product, but of the exchange of product,—a suggestion he has not himself heeded. It must give a simple and unified explanation of time value, wherever it is manifest. It must set in their true relation the theory of rent as the income from the use of goods in any given period, and interest as the agio or discount on goods of whatever sort, when compared throughout successive periods.[25]

---

24 The reader will observe that the term rent was there used in the more general sense of the income from the use, or the usance, of agents, not merely in the sense of contractual rent. This particular terminology, which was due to the influence of J.B. Clark, has since been modified not to weaken, but to strengthen the conception involved.

25 Frank Fetter, "The 'Roundabout Process' in the Interest Theory," *Quarterly Journal of Economics* 17, no. 1 (November, 1902): 179.

A year later, in 1903, I outlined the same conception of a thoroughgoing psychological analysis, and for the first time gave the name of "a theory of capitalization" to the proposed treatment of what usually is called "economic interest."

> Another solution may be found by combining into a logical system the three typical modes in which goods appeal to wants. First, goods appeal directly as want-gratifiers immediately available. Here is required a theory of wants and enjoyable goods, and the technical analysis of marginal utility. The mental process here examined is chronologically the first stage of evaluation, in the history both of the individual and of the race. Secondly, goods appear as more or less durable, and may be made comparable by being considered, through repairs, to be lasting use-bearers, yielding in a given short period a group of uses. Here is the place for the theory of rents. This is chronologically the second stage of evaluation, when durable goods are thought of and expressed in terms of their usufructs. Thirdly, whenever two nonsynchronous gratifications, rents or series of rents, are exchanged, they must be discounted to their present worth to be made comparable. Here is required a theory of capitalization, that is, of economic interest. This is historically as well as logically the latest stage of evaluation, characteristic of a developed money economy and of a "capitalistic" era. These three phases must be observed in every complete analysis of value.[26]

In an elementary textbook published in 1904 (*The Principles of Economics*) this conception of the interest theory was embodied, not as a thing apart from, but as an integral part of, a general theory of value. This mode of treatment, though new,[27]

---

26 Frank Fetter, "The Relations between Rent and Interest," *Publications of the American Economic Association*, 3rd series, 5, no. 1 (1904): 197; Papers and Proceedings of the Sixteenth Annual Meeting (December, 1903).

27 Believing this conception to be logically involved in much of Böhm-Bawerk's argument in his critical volume, "Capital and Interest," I credited him with "the fertile suggestion" (see above quotation from the article, "The Roundabout Process"). But he has not accepted this interpretation; indeed, this would invalidate the greater part of what is distinctive in his positive theory of the roundabout process, to which he adheres without change in the latest edition, 1912.

was not labeled with a distinctive name, and, being presented in an elementary text, has doubtless remained unread by many economists, and its true import unrecognized by some who have read it.

As is shown in the passages cited above, my conception long has been that in the analysis of the value problem the value of enjoyable goods must be first considered; that this should be followed by the valuation connected with the *physical productivity* of agents; and that only after full consideration of income expressed in psychic terms, in physical terms, and in monetary terms, is it in order to take up the theory of time-value, which is then to be developed as the basis of capitalization of incomes and of a resulting rate of contract interest.

Positive Statement of the Capitalization Theory

Accordingly, in my text, the first forty pages are devoted to psychic income and to the process of valuation which results in a price of things considered as directly enjoyable objects of choice. In the next division, comprising nearly sixty pages, is taken up the physical productivity of wealth, the uses of goods, and the valuation of those uses. Contract rent is here based upon the valuation, to individuals, of the productive uses of durable agents, just as contract price is based upon the valuation of enjoyable goods. A hundred pages were thus given to explaining, as well as I was able to do it in a first sketch of the theory of distribution for elementary students, what income is, and how income arises, so that it may be the object of choice and of exchange. In the next division (Capitalization and Time-value) I discussed, in seventy pages, the various problems of value that arise from a comparison of goods in point of time. I treated capitalization as the problem of valuation of durable agents, and developed a theory of the rate of interest on contract loans based on this conception of capitalization.

For the reader unacquainted with the capitalization theory, its essential features may be here outlined. At the outset let us seek to avoid the confusion caused by the use of the word interest in two senses, first, of a payment for contract loans made in terms of money, and, second, of the difference in value between like goods available at different times. Economists have of late generally recognized these two meanings, and have sought to distinguish them by the terms contract and economic interest.[28] Though such a terminology is an improvement upon the old, it leaves an ambiguity that continually reappears in the discussion. I therefore used the word interest solely in its original and still almost universal commercial sense of contract interest, and I used the term time-value to designate the other problem of "economic" or "implicit" interest.[29]

Seeing the two problems as in large measure distinguishable, and seeking for the logical starting point in the study, I asked: Which of these two questions was prior in history and which is primary in logic? In both cases the answer was time-value. The canon of priority in economic reasoning applied here: whichever of two interrelated problems or mutually acting forces can be thought of as existing without the other must be primary in the explanation. A rate of interest on money loans would be unthinkable if there were no differences relative to time in the estimates men placed on some goods available at different points of time. On the other hand, the use of money and the practice of borrowing and lending in terms of money are of comparatively recent origin; and the estimate of time-value today is thinkable, and is actually made, apart from the use of money or from any act of

---

28 Fisher prefers to call the one explicit and the other implicit interest. However, throughout his book he uses the phrase "the rate of interest" almost if not exclusively for contract interest, and other terms, such as rate of preference, time preference, etc., when implicit interest is meant.

29 Other expressions, to designate various aspects of the same problem, used in my *Principles of Economics* (New York: The Century Co., 1904), were "choice between different values," p. 104; "difference in want-gratifying power," p. 144; "time-difference," "time-discount," "the rate of time-discount," p. 145; "estimate of time value," p. 145; "a choice between present enjoyment and future provision," p. 146; "a premium rate on present goods," p. 146; "the exchange in time-valuation," p. 146; "preference of the future over the present," p. 158; "the preference of present over future," p. 159.

borrowing or exchange between persons. It must always have been found, as it now is in countless cases, in an impersonal relation between man and objects. Further, I applied the same test to determine the priority of capitalization and the rate of interest on loans (taking capitalization to mean simply putting a valuation, a present worth, upon a more or less durable group or source of incomes). The usual view has been that capitalization is subsequent to a rate of interest. But capitalization, as the process of putting a present worth upon any durable source of wealth and thus discounting its future uses by the act of exchanging it for other things, must have occurred many times before a rate of contract interest existed. This process surely occurs now in many cases without previous reference to such a rate. If, however, the less crude view be taken, that the interest problem studied is economic interest (time-discount) rather than contract interest, it is clear that this also is an aspect of the capitalization rather than antecedent to it. This rate of discount ("implicit" or "economic interest") is in itself nothing but an arithmetic reflection, in no sense causal, of the preference implied in the valuation of goods. Robinson Crusoe, in his individual economy, must, by his choice of goods which embody uses maturing at different periods, wrap up a scale of time-values which only later, if ever, except in a very vague form, appear as an arithmetic rate. The primitive economy in its choice of enjoyable goods of different epochs of maturity, in its wars for the possession of hunting grounds and pastures, in its slow accumulation of a store of valuable durable tools, weapons, houses, boats, ornaments, flocks and herds, first appropriated from nature, and then carefully guarded and added to by patient effort—in all this and in much else the primitive economy, even though it were quite patriarchal and communistic, without money, without formal trade, without definite arithmetic calculations, was nevertheless *capitalizing*, and therefore embodying in its economic environment a rate of premium and discount as between present and future.

This, then, is the essence of the capitalization theory of interest as nearly as we can put it in a proposition: The rate of interest (contractual) is the reflection, in a market price on money loans, of a rate of capitalization involved in the prices of the goods in the community. The price of durable agents is a capitalization which involves a discount of their future uses, and this is logically prior to the rate of contract interest. The logical order of explanation is from numberless separate acts of choice of goods *with reference to time*, to the value (and prices) of durable goods embodying future incomes, and finally to the market rate of interest.[30] This interest theory was new in its *order of development* from elementary choice; in the *priority it assigned to capitalization* above contract interest; in its *unified psychological explanation* of all the phenomena of the surplus that emerges when undervalued expected incomes approach maturity, the surplus all being derived from the value of enjoyable (direct) goods, not by two separate theories, for consumption and production goods respectively; in the *integration* of the interest theory *with the whole theory of distribution*; and in a number of details necessarily related to these features.

A just opinion of the newer theory is possible only to those who are willing to rethink the fundamental economic concepts. The change in the interest theory is only a part of the general reformulation of distributive theory which has been under way for a third of a century. It is to be understood only in that light.

---

30 When, however, attention is given to the details in the modern loan market following the action of this man or that, or studying a temporary situation such as a sudden demand for loans on the occasion of a war or in a financial panic, we break into the explanation at a different point. The change in the immediate status of the loan market is reflected in widening circles and for a time affects the capitalization of much of the wealth in the economy (of the nation or of the world). This and many other needed interpretations are briefly indicated in my elementary text. It is fundamental to the conception of the capitalization theory, however, that these impulses from the money market are not, as they superficially appear, primary or causal in a theory of interest, in the same sense as is the preference in time for enjoyable goods and the resulting level of capitalization. See especially chaps. 17–19 in my *Principles of Economics*.

Some Difficulties in Fisher's Impatience Theory

From the standpoint of the capitalization theory, the various questions raised in the discussion between Seager and Fisher and in Professor Brown's paper, appear from a new angle. It seems to be a different standpoint from that of Fisher, although at times he may appear to hold it. It is true that in his work *The Rate of Interest*, in which his theory was first presented, he introduced his "first approximation" with a chapter on time preference, which he declares to be "the central fact in the theory of interest," giving in a footnote without comment at this point[31] a page reference to my text. He says that "the income concept plays the central role."[32] But he treats capitalization as subsequent to a rate of interest, saying:

> When any other goods than enjoyment incomes are considered their values already imply a rate of interest. When we say that interest is the premium on the value of a present house over that of a future house we are apt to forget that the value of each is itself based on a rate of interest. We have seen that the price of a house is a discounted value of its future income. In the process of discounting there lurks a rate of interest. The value of houses will rise or fall as the rate of interest falls or rises. Hence, when we compare the values of present and future houses, both terms of the comparison involve the rate of interest. If, therefore, we undertake to make the rate of interest depend on the relative preference for present over future houses, we are making it to depend on two elements in each of which it already enters.[33]

And again he says, "The value of the capital is found by taking the income which it yields and capitalizing it by means of the rate of interest."[34] Still later he writes, "Capital value is merely the present or discounted value of income. But whenever we discount income we have to assume a rate of interest."[35]

---

31 Fisher, *Rate of Interest*, p. 88.
32 Ibid.
33 Ibid., p. 91.
34 Irving Fisher, *Elementary Principles* (New York: Macmillan, 1912), p. 229.
35 Ibid., p. 336.

From the moment Fisher begins his first approximation[36] he takes his standpoint in the money market and supposes an existing rate of interest to which rates of time preference of individuals are later brought into conformity. His treatment throughout is of the actuarial, mathematical type, concerned with the explaining and equalizing of incomes which are assumed to be present. I feel as strongly as does Professor Seager the neglect, in this treatment, of the element of productivity in accounting for the existence of the incomes.[37] From my point of view, the difficulty appears to inhere in Fisher's general conception of the problem.[38] I differ from the productivity theorist, however, in looking upon the interest problem as that of explaining not the existence nor yet the magnitude of those incomes, but the rate of their valuation to the valuation of the capital sum (principal) to which the contract rate (percentage) refers.

---

36 Fisher, *Rate of Interest*, p. 117.
37 Seager, (critique) "Impatience Theory of Interest," 836–37.
38 My purpose, in large part, in calling attention to my mode of approach to the interest problem as outlined above, is to show that the psychological theory, in its original form, is not open to the criticism which Seager forcibly directs against Fisher, "that he dissociates his discussion completely from any account of the production of wealth." To be sure, Fisher's reply ("Impatience Theory of Interest," 616), begins with a categorical denial, "I did not dissociate", but he immediately admits that in his "first approximation" the income streams were "temporarily assumed." And while in his larger theoretical book, he believes that "this assumption gives place to the more complicated conditions of the actual world," when he comes to the second and third approximations, he confesses that those complications were, "for the most part, omitted (as too difficult and controversial)" from the elementary book. Seager's comment ("Impatience Theory of Interest," 618) is pertinent: "A methodology that causes an author to drop out an essential link when he tries to restate his theory in elementary form seems to me to be almost self-condemned." At this point may be recalled my own criticism of Fisher's treatment of capital in his *Capital and Income*. Reviewing this in the *Journal of Political Economy* 15 (March, 1907): 147, I spoke of a "certain isolation in Fisher's capital theory. He began the analysis and reconstruction of the capital concept as if it were a task apart from the theory of distribution as a whole…. The capital theory presented has therefore a certain character of intellectual aloofness that leaves it out of touch with the larger theory of distribution, of which it should be but one part." The same criticism applies in general to *The Rate of Interest*, published a year later.

I share with Seager the opinion that there is no "sovereign virtue in mathematical modes of thought" which safeguards the mathematical economist from error. Indeed, there seem to be characteristic mathematical illusions.

I share Seager's doubt of the aptness of the proposition that impatience is "a fundamental attribute of human nature" or is "the essence of interest," though my doubts are for a different reason.[39] It is interesting to notice that Fisher himself did not seem to hold this view when he wrote *The Rate of Interest* in 1907. He said:

> It shows also that the preference for present over future goods of like kind and number is not, as some writers seem to assume, a necessary attribute of human nature, but that it depends always on the relative provisioning of the present and future.[40]

In an article in 1911, he for the first time used the term impatience in this connection, which he confesses is but a "catchword" in place of time preference. With this change of name has gone a change in the conception of the thing designated.

> In my own book, *The Rate of Interest*, for instance, this term was unused because unthought of, and the clumsier and less explanatory term "time-preference" was employed instead. The proposal to employ the term "impatience" is here made for the first time.... Impatience is a fundamental attribute of human nature.[41]

In 1912, he restates the same view: "It [impatience] is a fundamental attribute of human nature.... Interest is, as it were, human impatience crystallized into a market rate."[42]

My objection to this change of terms is that if the new word is more "catchy" it is less fitting than the word it displaces. Impatience is freighted with suggestions of "eagerness

---

39 Seager, (critique) "Impatience Theory of Interest," 835.
40 Fisher, *Rate of Interest*, p. 184.
41 Fisher, "Impatience Theory of Interest," 387.
42 Fisher, *Elementary Principles*, p. 371.

for change, restlessness, chafing of spirit, fretfulness, passion" (Webster). Time-valuation or time preference better expresses the complex of motives which at one time impels men to get goods earlier, and again leads them to postpone use by storing goods and by working for the future in many ways. A prevailing rate of interest is the resultant of all kinds and degrees of time preference in a community, *preference for goods in the future* in some cases, as well as preference for goods in the present, and it seems a great straining of words to attribute the resulting rate of interest to impatience alone. Patience, self-denial, the quality expressed in the old term abstinence, have a no less important part in the explanation.

Let us pass with brief mention the question which takes up a goodly space in Seager's criticism and in Fisher's reply—whether individuals are able to, and actually do, bring their "rate of impatience" (time preference) into exact accord with that implied in the market rate of interest. Seager did well to question the statement, and Fisher's concessions on this point do not leave very much in dispute. The individual brings his rate of time preference into accord with the market rate, so long as that adjustment yields him an advantage, and so far as he has something to exchange, can furnish security, or is not hindered by friction in other ways. Within the larger national economy, there are many imperfectly connected, provincial, class and family groups living in diverse economic conditions, and having diverse capitalization rates. In the central credit market, as in the simplest typical price problem of the sale of commodities, we may always conceive of some excluded would-be buyers, and likewise sellers, who remain outside the limits of actual trading because valuing their purchasing power and the sale-goods in a ratio which gives no margin of advantage at the market price.

Physical- and Value-Productivity Distinguished

The more serious theoretical issue involved here is the ground of Seager's objection, which Fisher does not touch in his reply.

It is that the technical productivity of agents is the cause of the impatience. Seager says:

> So far as I can see, with the technical superiority of present over future goods, or the productivity of capital, absent, the question as to whether interest would continue or not is an entirely open one.... Is it [time preference] not rather a result of the present industrial organization of society arising chiefly from the fact that capital plays such a tremendously important role in production and that, under the system of private property in the instruments of production and free competition, capitalists can secure a return corresponding, at least roughly, to the part of the value-product that is economically imputable to the assistance which their capital renders? That is the view of the productivity theorists.[43]

Whereupon Seager enters into a defense of the productivity theory, via a direct denial of Böhm-Bawerk's criticism of it as adopted by Fisher.[44]

Seager's argument at this point seems, indeed, to imply, as Fisher says, that Seager regards "all productivity theories as alike sound in principle."[45] Seager's opinion has, however, an element of progressiveness in it, for he says that nothing has shaken his "confidence in the essential soundness of the productivity-theory explanation of interest, when presented not as the complete explanation but as the necessary supplement to the discount theory."[46] He suggests in his explanation (also eclectic) of the way in which expenses of production and prices are related, that it is "nearer the truth to say that prices ... determine the expense of production than the reverse." Yet he concludes, "the chain of causation is not straight, but it turns upon itself in a

---

43 Seager, (critique) "Impatience Theory of Interest," 841–42.
44 Fisher has followed Böhm-Bawerk in presenting objections to the productivity theory in terms that logically invalidate every productivity theory and, apparently, is again following his example in withdrawing the objections in so far as they apply to any but the naïve theories. (See above, pp. 128–30.)
45 Brown, "Marginal Productivity versus Impatience Theory of Interest," 617.
46 Seager, (critique) "Impatience Theory of Interest," 849.

circle."[47] He seems about to avow the same doctrine of coordinate rank and mutual influence as between technical productivity and time preference, but he turns to the view that the part of productivity is in a fuller sense causal and primary, and that time-discount is the resultant of this.[48] He declares that it is borrowers' "demand for capital growing out of" the productivity which is "the positive, active influence determining interest."

The capitalization theorist is compelled regretfully to reject the compromise involved in this enlightened eclecticism. For this is the way Seager begins his indication of what his theory "does and what it does not involve":

> It starts out with the proposition that entrepreneurs desirous of making profits by supplying goods at current prices compete against one another for control of the factors necessary to production. This competition tends to keep their own profits down to a large or small "wages-of-management" and to force them to pass along as the remuneration of the factors which they hire, subject to this deduction and to a deduction for the replacement fund, the total price which they receive for the things which they sell. It is, therefore, contended that it is the part these factors play in production as compared and measured by the entrepreneurs that determines the shares of this total price that are assigned to them. The part that capital plays presents two aspects: that of capital goods available at a given instant of time, and that of the purchasing power tied-up in these capital goods during the period that they are performing their productive function. In relation to the first aspect, entrepreneurs appear as buyers. Normally, under conditions of free competition, the prices which they must pay for capital goods conform to their expenses of production. In relation to the interest they can afford to pay for such use, entrepreneurs estimate through comparing the productive services of capital goods at current prices with the productive services of workers, who at some points are interchangeable

---

47 Seager, (critique) "Impatience Theory of Interest," 845.
48 Ibid., 848.

with capital goods, at current rates of wages. Through these comparisons the general rate of interest, so far as it depends upon the demand for capital for use in production, is determined.[49]

Space does not permit of detailed comment to show that almost every sentence of this argument clashes with the physical productivity theory.

The productivity of which use is made when the explanation is really begun is not technical or physical productivity at all, but is the capacity which goods bought with judgment *at current prices* have, in the hands of enterprisers, of yielding a net surplus, sufficient not only to remunerate them, but to pay contract interest to lenders. The amount of interest which "enterprisers estimate" they can afford to pay (i.e., the maximum amount) is the difference between the discounted, or present, worth of products imputable to these agents and their worth at the time they are expected to mature. The prices of the agents, which are the costs, involve (not presuppose) a rate of discount. As was said in my text:

> When the agent is bought outright, the very concluding of the bargain fixes a relation between the expected value of the income and the value of the capital invested. In other words, the exchange of durable agents virtually wraps up in them a net income which it is expected will unfold year by year when rents mature and are secured.[50]

Undoubtedly, at this point is the crucial test of the competing theories. Is it productivity of agents that makes businessmen willing to borrow and pay interest? Could they afford to pay interest varying with the time element, if the value of the productivity, however large or small, were not discounted in the price of the agents they borrow (or buy with borrowed money)? I think not. Seager says:

---

49 Seager, (critique) "Impatience Theory of Interest," 847–48.
50 Fetter, *Principles of Economics*, p. 127.

> It is their [the businessmen's] demand for the savings of others for use in business enterprises that causes the balance always to be on the side of a positive rate of interest.[51]

But this demand cannot reasonably begin unless there is already a balance on the side of a discount of values of the future uses of agents. Viewed from the standpoint of the capitalization theory, the causal order is the reverse of that of the productivity theory. Of course, there must be future expected uses (incomes), that is, productivity, as there must be men if there is to be a valuation process, and as there must be some social organization if there are to be markets and prices. But if the future value of the products were not discounted, there could be no rate of interest. It varies with the magnitude of the time-discount at which borrowers, on the whole, are able to buy the title to the future products; and time-discount varies with changes in the whole complex economic situation, of which technical productivity is but one element, others being forethought, provision for needs in accordance with a prevailing standard (itself a complex thing), social and moral ideals, political conditions, etc., etc. It is the opportunity which the possession of ready money gives to the enterpriser to buy goods at a price involving a discount proportional to the futurity of the expected returns, that makes him willing to contract to pay interest. When these expected returns (the products) do appear in the course of time, their value-magnitude is, or should be, greater than was their investment magnitude, and it is out of this value-surplus, directly *conditioned on an antecedent discount of the value-productivity*, that contract interest is paid.

Before leaving this phase of our subject, let us look at it from one more angle, in the hope that some reader may find this a more helpful point of view. My contention throughout has been that the productivity theory in any of the versions known to me, and, specifically, in the entrepreneur version defended by Seager, involves a confusion between physical-productivity

---

51 Seager, (critique) "Impatience Theory of Interest," 838.

and value-productivity, that in the course of the reasoning there is a shift from the one idea to the other. Seager admits that this confusion "has sometimes occurred,"[52] but he believes that there is a "necessary or logical connection between physical-productivity *as a general phenomenon of capitalistic production* and value-productivity." To bridge this logical gap seems to him, however, to be so simple a task that express proof of it may be assumed "to be superfluous," for he thinks it is merely "an obvious deduction from the accepted principles in regard to the determination of exchange values and prices." His proposition, therefore, is substantially this: The capital (agents), by virtue of its technical productivity here and now, produces more goods, and these goods have (when commodities generally are considered, and not some exceptional commodity) a greater value than the goods which would have been obtained without the capital. Hence, Seager concludes:

> Admitting the physical-productivity of capital … the value-productivity … or more accurately an increase in the total value-product as a consequence of the assistance which capital renders to production seems to me to follow as a logically necessary consequence.[53]

Here, where Seager would expect dissent, I readily agree, but hasten to add that *this* value-productivity is not at all *that* of which the productivity theorist speaks in his interest theory. Here we are saying merely: If agents used at this moment produce more, the products (speaking of the general and usual result) have more value here and now than the products that could have been obtained without the help of the productive agents. But the value-productivity which furnishes the motive to the enterpriser to borrow and gives him the power, regularly, to pay contract interest, is due, not to the fact that these products will have value when they come into existence, but to the fact that their expected value is discounted in the price of the

---

52 Seager, (critique) "Impatience Theory of Interest," 842.
53 Ibid., 842–43.

agents bought at an earlier point of time. The two relations are in different planes. It is a problem of two dimensions which may be represented as follows:

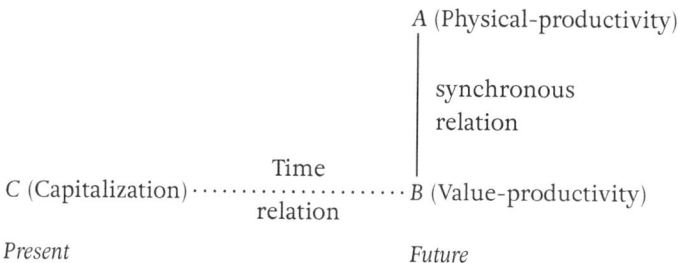

The modern productivity theorist assumes as quite obvious the value-productivity B, as derived synchronously from the physical-productivity A, but he ignores the problem of the discount relation in time between B and C. The pseudo-value-productivity assumed in the productivity theory of interest is all, however, involved in the unexplained discount relation between B and C, not in the identity relation between A and B. This is the *petitio principii* of the theory.

The value-surplus referred to is that part imputable to, and varying with, the time element, and not that due to the peculiar commercial skill, or to the luck, of the enterpriser in finding unusually low-valued agents in one place, or unusually high-valued products in another. If one did not bear in mind the complex character of the gross income "profits," one might be tempted to exclaim: If the enterpriser must pay as interest the whole amount involved in time-discount, he never would have a motive to borrow. It is just here that appears so plainly the middleman's character of the productive borrower. The rate of interest is a market price at which (security, etc., equalized) the individual borrows; but those with superior knowledge and superior foresight are able to buy in one economic group and to sell their products in another, to buy "underestimated" goods and to find a favorable market for highly esteemed products. They are merchants, buying when they can in a cheaper and selling in a dearer capitalization market,[54] acting as the equalizers of rates and prices. It is the mercantile function everywhere to do this. So we must dissent again when Seager says:

> And it is this demand for capital growing out of the important role capital plays as a factor in production, that is the positive, active influence determining interest, in the same sense that utility may be said to be the positive, active influence determining value.[55]

Rather, this demand for capital determines interest in the same sense that the merchant's demand determines the wholesale price of merchandise, he merely judging and transmitting to the wholesaler and manufacturer the ultimate consumer's demand for various goods. In this case, the middleman's demand for capital (that is, for loans) is a reflection of the time-valuation of consumers as embodied in the prices prevailing in the markets for goods.

Professor Seager seems so near at times to abandoning the cost-of-production theory of prices with which the productivity theory of interest is related, and has contributed such valuable and needed criticism to the present discussion, that it is to be hoped that he may yet bring his powerful aid to the capitalization camp.

The Capital Concept in the Interest Theory

The difficulty of seeing the capitalization problem in a broad way, as something touching all sources and groups of income, is, however, insurmountable so long as one adheres to the old concept of capital. Seager uses capital "in the sense of the produced means of further production,"[56] and distinguishes land and capital as two groups of concrete objects, one of which owes its value to nature, and the other to labor. It is, of course, futile to attempt

---

54 See above, pp. 138–40, 144–46.
55 Seager, (critique) "Impatience Theory of Interest," 848.
56 Ibid., 844.

here a restatement of the reasons, negative and positive, against this view. They have been pretty fully stated elsewhere. Seager seems still to conceive of the interest problem as connected only with produced means of production, as did the older English economists, and as all productivity theorists incline to do. This inclination is found along with a treatment limited mainly, if not entirely, to contract interest.

But how can the "economic interest" aspect of the problem be limited to the income yielded by tools and machines? Why is not this problem presented in the case of incomes from land (or from an orchard, to which example Seager objects as not being typical of all forms of capital)? How account for the capitalization of this land and of this orchard? By applying a rate of interest derived from the money market as Fisher would seem to do, or a rate taken from the market for the loan of purely "produced" capital goods (whatever that may mean)? Cannot unproduced agents be capitalized unless the rate of discount is first discovered by making produced goods? Is not a capitalization rate conceivable in a community where land is the only form of wealth that is bought and sold? If so, then the thought is not avoidable that a rate of interest on contract loans to purchase land may prevail, reflecting this implied rate of capitalization—the chance for profit operating as a motive for the loan just as it does in manufacturing and commerce. Is interest not connected with a loan of money to buy "natural" agents as fully as with that to buy "artificial" agents? An answer to these questions inevitably carries one into the atmosphere of the capitalization theory, where the arbitrary limitation of the interest problem to loans made to buy "produced" agents becomes unthinkable.

But there is still the old question, how account for the tendency of profits (in the old broad sense of the term, including interest) toward equality; how explain the fact that on the average, though with many exceptions and fluctuations, the rates of profit to be had by productive borrowers in the various industries do not get so very far apart? There is the old explanation of cost-of-production of capital, upon which the latest productivity theorists still rely, and there is the capitalization theory. Both of these concede a place to the enterpriser. In the older view, the place is worthy to be called causal, in that, when any agent yields an abnormal return, he produces more agents, by incurring "costs" (which are either assumed to be fixed or are left quite unexplained), putting the price of more labor and materials into them and thus bringing their price into conformity with other agents of the same cost. The citadel where the productivity theorist feels his position to be impregnable is just here, in the thought that the amount and the value of "capital" (produced agents) is "brought into conformity with the expense of producing them," thus regulating the interest rate. Seager is on familiar ground when he says:

> Since there is nothing in the assumption that the productivity of all instruments is doubled that involves any serious change in the expense of producing the instruments.[57]

We must dissent. The doubling of the productivity of all agents alike would have very diverse effects upon the prices of the various enjoyable goods, and these prices would be reflected in the valuation process to the prices of the different natural sources and of all other agents, thus altering greatly the whole scale of costs in "producing" more agents.

But is this not a recognition that technical productivity has some influence upon the comparison of present and future gratifications, and hence upon the rate of interest? Surely, some influence it has, but the causal order of explanation is very different from that of the productivity theory. Technical productivity is one of the facts, physical, moral, intellectual, which go to make up the whole economic situation in which time preference is exercised. That this, however, is not going over to the productivity theory of interest is shown by the fact that it points to an opposite conclusion as regards the resulting rate. The greater provision for present desires thus made possible leads us to expect a

---

57 Seager, (critique) "Impatience Theory of Interest," 847.

reduction of the preference for present goods and a lowering of their valuation in terms of future goods. This (other things being equal) would be reflected in a lower rate of time discount and a lower, not a higher, rate of interest, as the productivity theorist believes.[58]

May we not then conclude that the cost-of-production-of-capital explanation of interest is a partial glimpse of an intermediate and subordinate process of the adjustment of prices, in part a mistaking of effect for cause? It assumes a dual theory of investment prices; some prices are explained as due to demand and others as due to cost. The prices of the factors (materials, tools, labor) are taken as a basis from which to calculate the rate of interest, a sort of turtle's back (as in the ancient theory of the universe) on which the giant, Entrepreneur, stands while carrying on his back the burden of interest.

The capitalization theory views the causal order very differently. First, time-valuation being embodied in durable agents with incomes extending over a period of time becomes the capitalization of agents containing future uses, this involving a rate of time-discount. This, in a market with exchange, becomes price, which is cost to the enterpriser seeking a profit by buying these factors, combining them more or less with his own services, and selling them. This process is constantly levelling down inequalities in capitalization as between different commodities and markets. All men together are helping to evaluate all of the economic goods in the community. Within this larger circle of explanation, the part of the enterpriser is secondary and intermediate. He does not represent any additional "technical productivity" cause, coming in alongside of the psychological explanation of interest. The chance of income for himself exists before he makes a move, partly because the future incomes have already been discounted (the pure capital-income aspect), and partly because all agents are not discounted at any moment at exactly the same, or exactly

---

[58] On this Fisher has taken a position in accordance with the capitalization theory. See Fisher, (reply) "Impatience Theory if Interest," 614.

the right, rate (the commercial profit aspect). It is because of the chance of private profit already inherent in the situation that the producer is led to act in his intermediary capacity.

The Same Difficulties Again

The article by Professor H.G. Brown,[59] a former pupil and present colleague of Fisher, appeared almost simultaneously with Fisher's concessions to the productivity theory. Professor Brown, agreeing almost completely with Seager, formulates an eclectic theory.

> The position taken by the present writer is, that productivity and impatience are coordinate determinants, i.e., that productivity is as direct a determinant of interest as is impatience, and that productivity may be, in a modern community, the more important determinant.[60]

At every point where Professor Fisher is at his best, and rejects productivity "as a direct acting cause," Professor Brown disagrees with him, and accepts productivity. Yet the article is marked by a number of just observations and seems at one point to touch upon the truth of the capitalization theory:

> We may say that a person's valuation of capital, along with the valuations of other persons in like situation, is less the direct result of the previously existing market rate of interest, than it is, by affecting his and their attitude toward the market, a determinant of the rate of interest.[61]

But the argument on the whole is on the plane of that conception of productivity criticised above. Every feature of the old

---

59 Cited above, p. 127.
60 Brown, "Marginal Productivity versus Impatience Theory of Interest," 634. Here impatience and productivity are said to be coordinate determinants, though productivity may be the more important; and again, page 645, impatience is said "to enter into the chain of cause and effect" in a certain connection "as effect rather than cause"; and, finally, page 650, impatience "is also, to some extent, a joint consequence, with interest, of the other cause, the superiority of indirect production."
61 Ibid., 644.

argument is reproduced. The explanation is hardly begun until the productivity is assumed to be a 5 percent, a 10 percent, or a 20 percent productivity. Percent of what? Of the capital valuation, or the prices at which the borrower can buy the agents. Productivity in what way? In that the present prices, being the discounted value of the incomes that are expected, emerge at their maturing value as time elapses. The discount-rate involved in the capitalization is the "rate of productivity" which appears again and again in the argument. The borrower pays contract interest of 5 percent only when he thinks he sees the opportunity to get this increment and something more for his trouble. Simple and true as an explanation of why men borrow at a rate of contract interest related to the prevailing rate of time-discount, but no proof whatever that the rate of interest is due to technical productivity.

Here, as always, the productivity theorist looks at the proximate influence, not at that one step removed; examines the middleman's motive, and ignores the ultimate consumer. The productive borrower is but the intermediary, transmitting to the market of consumers through the agency of prices, the effects of time preference. Forgetting the motives and influences of the really determining group of minds, Professor Brown looks only at the "productive" borrower and says: "In what possible sense can it be said that he borrows only because he is impatient?"[62] "All question of impatience aside";[63] "For even those [productive borrowers] who are not by nature impatient" etc.[64] Professor Brown shows well[65] the inaptness of the word "impatience," but his argument is futile as a refutation of a true psychological theory, for he is quite overlooking the substance, while he chases the shadow, of time preference.

This motive to borrow exists as well when the agent to be bought with borrowed money is land, as when it is another agent.

---

62 Brown, "Marginal Productivity versus Impatience Theory of Interest," 638.
63 Ibid., 639.
64 Ibid., 640.
65 Ibid., 637.

But just here Professor Brown withdraws to the citadel, the cost-of-production of capital, as that which tends "to fix the rate of interest and of discount." He reaffirms the

> importance of the distinction which Professor Seager has recently emphasized, between land and made capital, between original natural resources and "the produced means to further production." Land is already present. For the most part, there is no balancing of choice as to whether or not we shall produce it.[66]

What is the force of "already present"? Does "for the most part there is no balancing of choice" etc., mean that the way we use land has not affected its quantity in the past, and does not affect it for the future, either as acres or as productive power? In this day of the conservation and reclamation movements, are we to forget the part of repairs and depreciation, and assume the immutability of acres, arable and other kinds? Is there not involved in any standard of husbandry where soil-fertility is maintained, an adjustment of the cost-of-production and of the capitalization of each arable acre to its price based on its expected return quite as this is done in the case of factories?[67]

It is not for us here to discuss further the older conception of capital here involved. We had supposed that it had become unthinkable in the atmosphere of Columbia and of Yale, under the influences of J.B. Clark and of Irving Fisher.

Summary

Surely we are making some progress in formulating more clearly the issues involved in the interest problem. The opinions we have reviewed face in at least three different directions, not squarely

---

66 Brown, "Marginal Productivity versus Impatience Theory of Interest," 644.
67 Professor V.G. Simkhovitch's illuminating article "Hay and History" (*Political Science Quarterly* 28, no. 3 [September, 1913]: 385–403) gives new evidence of the effect upon agricultural industry of enlarging man's power over the production of fertile and arable qualities in land.

opposing each other.[68] Seager and Brown stand together on one side of the circle of opinion, glancing now and then with one eye at a psychological explanation (for consumption loans) and with the other eye fixed most of the time on the enterpriser-productivity explanation. They are not far away from Böhm-Bawerk, who is likewise eclectic; but their conception of productivity goes little farther than the personal enterpriser, whereas Böhm-Bawerk seeks, though vainly, in his roundabout theory, to extend his explanation formally to the impersonal productive powers in the agents. Nearly opposite them stands Fisher, directing his attention mainly upon the market for money loans, but giving many glances before and after to the psychological causes, in accord with the capitalization theory. The capitalization theorist at another point in the circle is faced directly toward the psychological explanation of interest, and sees the other features of the picture in due perspective to this central fact.

Seen from any of these standpoints, the interest paid on *consumption* loans is and must be explained in purely psychological terms. The capitalization theory, alone, is not eclectic, and explains interest on consumption and on production loans, in the same psychological terms. It alone sees the enterpriser's part embraced within the larger circle of time preference, and explains interest on productive loans as but the reflection of the time preference in the minds of the great body of buyers in the community, whose representatives and intermediaries the enterprisers are.

---

68 A different conception, apparently a unique variation of the enterpriser-productivity theory, is the dynamic theory of Professor Schumpeter, as presented in his *Theorie der Wirtschaftlichen Entwicklung* (1912), and reviewed at length by Böhm-Bawerk in the *Zeitschrift für Volkswirtschaft* (1913).

Professor Rothbard
and the Theory of Interest

{ *By Roger W. Garrison* }

The Theory of Interest in Perspective

It has become increasingly true that individual economists are categorized in accordance with their chosen fields of specialization—regulation, for instance, or theory of finance, or monetary theory. Economists become known for some special insight or assumption that sets their analysis apart from the analyses of others—rent-seeking behavior, the efficient-market hypothesis, or so-called rational expectations. Name recognition and professional stature are directly proportional to the single-mindedness of the approach and to the extremes to which the economist is willing to push the analysis.

Students of economics have little difficulty grasping these special insights—unless the doggedness with which their expositors flush out implausible implications lead to a questioning of the underlying kernels of truth. The difficulties come in understanding how all these separate insights fit together into

---

Reprinted by *Man, Economy, and Liberty*, Walter Block and Llewellyn H. Rockwell, eds. (Auburn; Ala.: Ludwig von Mises Institute, 1988). The references that Professor Garrison appended to the original article are contained in the bibliography at the end of the book.

a coherent view of the economy. Rational expectations and the political business cycle, for example, are difficult to reconcile. The easy way out, students soon discover, is to pick a field, focus on an idea within the field, and leave the rest to others. Increased specialization, though, comes at the cost of a comprehension of and appreciation for economics more broadly conceived.

Professor Rothbard has provided for students a more rewarding, but more demanding, alternative—a coherent and comprehensive treatment of man, economy, and state. His treatise on economics offers a well integrated view of economic relationships, one that ignores artificial boundaries that confine the specialists to their own sub-disciplines. His writings taken as a whole advance the level of integration still further. The economics of liberty meshes with the ethics of liberty, and together they help us to understand the history of a country that was conceived in liberty. Although economics, ethics, and history are distinct disciplines in academe, Professor Rothbard has regarded them as different perspectives within a single discipline. By repackaging his ideas as libertarian studies, he has provided a coherent and comprehensive world view.

Thus, a full appreciation of Professor Rothbard's achievement requires that we recognize the breadth of his contribution. It is with some reluctance, then, that I narrow the focus of attention in order to consider the Austrian theory of interest and Professor Rothbard's treatment of it. It is as if we were to try to appreciate the handiwork of a highly skilled stonemason by focusing upon a particular stone. But at least we have picked an interesting and revealing stone: You tell me your theory of interest, and I'll have a good guess about the rest of your economics. Interest is just another word for profit? You're a Ricardian. To collect interest is to exploit labor? You're a Marxian. The interest rate is wholly determined by the growth rate of capital? You're a Knightian. Interest is fundamentally a monetary phenomenon? You're a Keynesian.

Professor Rothbard is none of these. This much is not in dispute. The controversy comes when we begin to distinguish

Rothbardians from Fisherians. Are time preferences of market participants and capital productivity independent co-determinants of the rate of interest, as Irving Fisher would have it? Or does time preference alone—the systematic discounting of the future—account for the payment that we call interest?

This latter view, which is properly attributed to Ludwig von Mises, is adopted by Professor Rothbard. Borrowing phraseology from Milton Friedman, it might be claimed that interest is always and everywhere a time-preference phenomenon in the same sense that inflation is always and everywhere a monetary phenomenon. Rothbard's defense of the time-preference theory of interest and his use of the theory as a building block in his treatise on economics inspires the remainder of this essay.

Productivity of the Factors

Those who have learned their interest theory from Professor Rothbard have learned to be suspicious about the use—the many uses—of the word "productive" in the literature on distributive shares, or factor imputation. The factors of production (land, labor, and capital) are employed in some combination to produce output. The idea that the factors are considered to be "productive" is indissociable from our understanding of what the factors are and what they can do. But using the term in this sense has no specific implications about the value of the separate factors or about the phenomenon of interest.

An additional dose of one of the factors of production, the other factors being employed in unchanged quantities, will allow for an increase in output. Each factor is productive at the margin. This marginal productivity, measured in value terms, has important implications about the prices of the factors—the price of an acre of land, of an hour's labor, or of the services of a capital good. Through the pricing mechanism, the value of the output is imputed to the individual factors in accordance with the values of their marginal products. The process of imputation, however, has no simple or direct bearing on questions concerning the rate of interest. The relationship between factor prices and the interest rate will be discussed at greater length in subsequent sections.

Does one of the factors of production allow for an output whose value exceeds the combined values of the factors of production? If such a factor exists, it would be productive in a very special sense. This factor would produce *surplus* value. If the search for the source of a supposed surplus value is confined to questions concerning the nature of the individual factors of production, the possible answers are few in number. A survey of the different positions taken, however, is revealing. Without digging very deep into the history of economic thought, we can find four points of view that, collectively, exhaust the possibilities.

François Quesnay believed that only land was capable of producing a surplus. The inherent productive powers of the soil allow for a given quantity of corn—employed as seed and worker sustenance—to be parlayed into a greater quantity of corn. The notion of land's natural fecundity lies at the root of Physiocratic thought.

Karl Marx believed that only labor can produce surplus value. Without labor, nothing at all can be produced. This one factor, then, is the ultimate source of all value. Income received by other factors represents not the productivity of those factors, but the exploitation of labor.

Frank Knight believed that there is only one factor of production and that it should be called capital. Rather than argue in terms of a factor that yields a surplus, he argued in terms of a stock that yields a flow. Capital consists of all inputs that have the dimensions of a stock (land, machines, human capital); the corresponding flow is the annual output net of maintenance costs. This net yield is a consequence of capital productivity. The net yield divided by the capital stock is the rate of interest.

Joseph Schumpeter, following Léon Walras, denied that there was any surplus to be explained. In long-run general equilibrium, the sum of the values imputed to the several factors of production must fully exhaust the value of the economy's output. Schumpeter insisted that in the long run, the interest rate must be zero; the positive rate of interest that we actually observe is to be understood as a disequilibrium phenomenon.

We can pause at this point for a midterm exam: Which of the factors of production is *truly* productive? (*a*) Land; (*b*) Labor; (*c*) Capital; (*d*) None of the above. Quesnay, Marx, Knight, and Schumpeter would answer (*a*), (*b*), (*c*), and (*d*), respectively. Professor Rothbard would reject the question. The notion of productivity in this sense—and hence the issue of the source of such productivity—vanishes once we take adequate account of the temporal pattern of inputs and outputs and of the effects of time preference on their relative values.

Analogies, Time Preference, and the *Pons Asinorum*

Analytical constructions that pass as theories of capital and interest are, in many instances, question-begging analogies. Hardtack is nonperishable; sheep multiply; a Crusonia plant grows. The rates of growth of these things—zero for hardtack—are dimensionally similar to the rate of interest. The interest rate is based on the comparison of the value of output net of inputs to the value of the inputs. It is tempting to think of the implied growth in *value* as being analogous to the *physical* growth rates of sheep or of Crusonia plants. But does the analogy hold? If not, then the economics of an all-sheep economy or of a Crusonia plant will result in a hopeless conflation of interest rates and growth rates.

Such analogies serve to obscure what the phenomenon of time preference can illuminate. According to Menger's Law, the value of ends is imputed to the means that make those ends possible. But if the end, the final output of a production process, lies in the future, its current value will be discounted in the minds of market participants. The general preference in the market for output sooner over output later has—or should have—the same status as the general preference for more output over less output. Market participants discount the future. The extent to which a particular individual discounts it depends upon his own time preferences, which in turn depend upon his particular circumstances.

Currently existing means are valued in the marketplace in accordance with the *discounted* value of the corresponding (future) ends. Because of this discounting, the total value of the currently existing factors of production falls short of the value of the future output that these factors make possible. It would be misleading to claim that there is a "growth" in value between the employment of inputs and the emergence of output. And the value difference (between output and inputs) does not constitute a "surplus" in any meaningful sense.

The existence of (positive) time preferences—the general preference for achieving ends sooner over achieving them later—is both necessary and sufficient for the emergence of the market phenomenon called interest. If market participants were characterized by a general indifference about when their ends are achieved, about the remoteness in time of output, then the value of the means, of inputs, would reflect the full, undiscounted value of their contribution to the production of output. There would be no value difference, no interest return to account for. If market participants do discount the future, then the value of present inputs will be systematically less than the value of future output. The value difference is interest.

These propositions hold for all production processes. The inputs may grow in some literal, biological sense into outputs, or the inputs may be converted into outputs by means of some technologically advanced—or technologically backward—production process. Indeed, with appropriate changes in wording, these propositions that establish (positive) time preference as a necessary and sufficient condition for the emergence of interest in a production economy can be applied to a pure-exchange economy as well: Goods promised for future delivery will exchange at a discount for goods presently available.

The time-preference theory of interest provides us not only with a firm understanding of the phenomenon of interest but also with a *pons asinorum*, or acid test, for productivity theories of whatever variety. A particular input, or factor, may be productive, maybe even especially productive, in some sense. There is no simple relationship, however, between this productivity and the phenomenon of interest. The critical question is tirelessly posed by Professor Rothbard: Why is the ability of this factor to produce not fully reflected in its market price?

The answer, of course, is that the discounting is a direct implication of the existence of time preferences. The output which this productive factor helps to produce lies in the future. The market value of the factor itself, then, is discounted accordingly. An argument that a particular factor is highly productive may explain why its price is as high as it is, but it does not and cannot explain why its price is not higher still. That is, productivity does not and cannot explain why the factor's price fails to exhaust the undiscounted contribution to the production of output.

Is the Interest Rate the Price of a Factor Called "Waiting"?

Somewhere between the time-preference theory of interest and the alternative theories already mentioned lies the view that the interest rate is the price of a factor of production called "waiting." The notion of waiting or abstinence as the basis for interest payments has a rich history and predates the Austrian School and its time-preference theory. Abstinence was treated as a "real cost" in Nassau Senior's nineteenth-century analysis. Waiting, or abstinence in a more abstract sense, figured heavily in the turn-of-the-century writings of Gustav Cassel and of John B. Clark and in the subsequent writings of Frank Knight. In recent years Leland Yeager, following Cassel, has directed our attention once again to the centrality of the concept of waiting in theories of interest-rate determination.

Although theorizing in terms of time preferences and theorizing in terms of the factor of production called waiting can yield the same conclusions, the Austrians have not fully embraced this alternative mode of analysis. Eugen von Böhm-Bawerk was critical of Cassel's formulation; Friedrich Hayek considered Knight's productivity theory to be counterproductive; and Israel Kirzner has taken issue with modern reformulations. Neither Mises nor Rothbard has specifically addressed the question of waiting as a factor of production, but passages can be found in the writings of each suggesting that the time-preference view and the waiting-as-a-factor view are to some extent compatible. It may be worthwhile, then, to consider the kinship between the two views.

Cassel was careful to point out that the word "waiting" is not being used with its ordinary dictionary meaning. Waiting as a factor of production and waiting for a bus are two different things. In fact, they are even *dimensionally* different. The latter is measured strictly in units of time; the former is measured in compound units that account for both value and time. More specifically, Casselian waiting is the product of value and time and is measured in dollar-years (or $-years). Thus, an individual who forgoes the spending of $100 for a period of two years supplies (neglecting the effects of compounding) 200 $-years of waiting. This constitutes more waiting than a second individual who forgoes the spending of only $75 for the same two years, and more waiting than a third individual who forgoes the spending of $50 for three years.

The issue of units is a critical one not only for understanding what waiting means and how it is measured, but also for checking the dimensional conformability between waiting as a factor and the interest rate as its price. The price of any factor is measured in terms of dollars per unit of the factor. Land rent is measured in $/(acre-year); the wage rate in $/(worker-hour); the service price of a capital good, say a machine, in $/(machine-hour). The interest rate is measured in frequency units, in inverse time. That is, the dimensions of the interest rate are 1/year—e.g., 10 percent *per year*. Any attempt to recast the interest rate as the price of a factor must be squared with this dimensional characteristic.

It can be seen immediately that the interest rate cannot be the price—or even the service price—of capital goods. The dimensions of $/machine—or of $/(machine-hour)—are not the same as the units of the interest rate. Nor can waiting in the ordinary dictionary sense be the thing whose price is the interest rate. The price of waiting in this sense would be measured in $/year.

But the concept of waiting introduced by Cassel and adopted by Yeager is measured in $-years. The price of Casselian waiting, then, is measured in units of $/($-year), or, simplifying, in units of 1/year. Thus, the claim that waiting is a factor of production whose price is the rate of interest squares with the fact that the interest rate is measured in units of inverse time. It should be argued, though, that the interest rate is determined by the supply and demand for waiting whether or not the waiting is employed as a factor of production. In fact, this argument can be seen as no more than a generalization of the fact that the more narrowly conceived loan rate of interest is determined by the supply and demand for loans. Loans, whether to producers or consumers, have both a value and a time dimension, are measured in units of $-years, and constitute one form of waiting. Theorizing in terms of waiting—whatever particular form it may take—serves to emphasize the pervasiveness of the phenomenon of interest. And this emphasis is characteristic of the writings of both Yeager and Rothbard.

The generalizing from loans to waiting, however, introduces some analytical difficulties. Marshallian partial-equilibrium analysis applies in its conventional way to the market for loans. Shifts in the supply or in the demand for loans can be analyzed on the basis of the familiar *ceteris paribus* assumption: Prices in other markets, such as factor markets, are assumed not to change. The *ceteris paribus* assumption breaks down, though, when the analysis is extended from the market for loans to the general phenomenon of waiting. This is only to say that partial-equilibrium analysis cannot be applied in any straightforward way to an all-pervasive economy-wide phenomenon. The particular difficulties introduced can be illustrated with a simple example.

Suppose the current rate of interest (the price of waiting) is 5 percent and that the equilibrium quantity of waiting supplied and demanded is 1000 $-years, which consists of owning durable machines, whose current value is $1000 for one year. Now suppose that the demand for waiting increases. Simple supply-and-demand analysis would allow us to predict that the interest rate will rise, say from 5 to 10 percent, and that the quantity of waiting supplied and demanded will increase.

If the value of the machines could be assumed not to change, this prediction would be valid. But a rise in the interest rate will cause the value of the machines, which is simply the discounted value of the machines' future output, to fall. More specifically, the doubling of the rate of interest, which serves as the basis for the discounting, will cause the value of the machines to decrease from $1,000 to $500. Owning those same machines for a year now constitutes only half the waiting. It is possible, then, that in the subsequent equilibrium, more machines will be owned for a longer period of time, yet the amount of waiting, which is now based on a lower machine price, may be less than in the initial equilibrium.

The ambiguity identified in the example is unavoidable. The amount of waiting increases as we move up the supply schedule because of the nature of the supply relationship, but it decreases as the interest rate rises because of the way waiting is linked computationally to factor prices, which in turn are affected by changes in the rate of interest. There is no ambiguity, however, about the direction of change in the rate of interest given a particular shift in supply or in demand. An increase in the demand for waiting, which is the same thing as a rise in time preferences, will cause the rate of interest to rise.

Thus, the view that the interest rate is determined by the supply and demand for waiting is compatible with the view that it is determined by time preferences. But the waiting-as-a-factor theory strains our intuition about the meaning of waiting, involves unavoidable ambiguities about the direction of changes in the "amount" of waiting, and adds little to our understanding of the phenomenon of interest. Occam's Razor provides a clear basis for favoring the time-preference theory embraced by Professor Rothbard.

The Eclectic View: Time Preference and Capital Productivity

The comparison of the waiting-as-a-factor view and the time-preference view paves the way for a summary assessment of the more conventional treatment of interest-rate determination. Following Irving Fisher, modern textbooks make use of a two-period model which includes a convex intertemporal opportunity curve and a family of concave intertemporal indifference curves. The slope of the opportunity curve is intended to represent the marginal productivity of capital; the slope of the indifference curves represents the marginal rate of time preference. Self-interest and unhampered markets are enough to assure that the actual intertemporal pattern of consumption is the one represented by the point at which an indifference curve is tangent to the opportunity curve. The slope at the point of tangency reflects the equilibrium rate of interest.

Time preferences and the productivity of capital, then, are depicted as independent co-determinants of the market rate of interest. Neither co-determinant, by itself, is capable of determining anything. And the question of which determinant is the more decisive is, at best, a question of the relative degrees of curvature. To illustrate the polar cases, if either the indifference curves or the opportunity curve is a straight line, then the slope of the straight line will determine the rate of interest no matter where on that line the point of tangency occurs.

The Fisherian analytics are simple enough, but the basic construction is conceptually flawed. Again, the issue of dimensions comes into play. The slope of the indifference curves has the dimensions of the interest rate ($1/year$). The slope of the opportunity curve must be dimensionally the same if the point of tangency is to have any intelligible meaning at all. If the slope is a marginal value product, then it must be the marginal value product of *waiting*, not of *capital*. But as demonstrated in the previous section, the quantity of waiting is itself dependent upon factor prices, which in turn are dependent upon the interest rate. It cannot legitimately be argued, then, that the rate of interest has two independent co-determinants; one of those co-determinants is dependent upon the magnitude it supposedly helps to determine.

Modern textbook writers have attempted to skirt this problem by using a one-good model. In all such models, questions of value, which may be affected by changes in the rate of interest, simply do not arise. Value productivity and physical productivity are indistinct; productivity is modelled as the rate of increase in the quantity of the good. The phenomenon of interest is being analogized once again to sheep that reproduce or to plants that grow. But, as Professor Rothbard often reminds us, the rate of interest is a ratio of values, not of quantities. This modeling technique unavoidably conflates growth rates with interest rates and fails thereby to shed any light on the phenomenon of interest.

It is interesting to note that Fisher himself clearly acknowledged the actual interdependency of the two co-determinants, but he seemed not to realize the problem that this poses for the eclectic view. Once it is understood that the opportunity curve incorporates interest-rate considerations, the time-preference view comes into its own. The formal demonstration that the equilibrium rate of interest is given by the slope of the tangency in a Fisher diagram can be easily reconciled with the Mises-Rothbard view. The equilibrium rate, which on grounds of logical consistency must reflect both time preferences and the rate of discount on which the opportunity curve is based, is to be attributed to the interaction of market participants who systematically discount the future. That is, the rate of interest is simply the market's reflection of time preferences.

The rejection of the idea that the Fisher diagram identifies two independent co-determinants does not mean that the diagram is totally without meaning. And the recognition that time preferences are represented on both sides of the tangent suggests a particular reinterpretation. The family of indifference curves can retain their conventional interpretation. At the point of tangency, the opportunity curve depicts the time preferences of market participants as currently embodied in the economy's capital structure. Points on the opportunity curve to either side of the point of tangency depict the extent to which the capital structure can be modified so as to alter the time pattern of output in each direction.

This reinterpretation is consistent with that of Hayek, who went on to argue that the slope of the opportunity curve at a given point may depend upon which direction market forces are pushing. More specifically, he argued that once the construction of a particular capital structure is underway, the opportunities for producing output sooner than initially planned may be severely limited. But employing Fisherian analytics to illustrate the limited modifiability of the economy's capital structure is not at all at odds with the time-preference theory of interest.

A Summary Assessment

Theories of capital and interest are considered by many to be the most difficult theories in the discipline of economics. The difficulties stem in large part from the multiple meanings of productivity and from the issue of units—the fact that the quantity of capital or the quantity of waiting is reckoned in terms of its own price. Biological and botanical analogies have added confusion. Their deceptively simple answers come at the cost of losing sight of the question. Propositions about growth rates cannot be translated in any direct way into propositions about interest rates.

The Fisher diagram has its uses. This is not to be denied. And the payment of interest can be accounted for in terms of the supply and demand for waiting. But these conceptual contrivances mask more than they reveal. Those who have learned their capital and interest theory from *Man, Economy, and State* should be able to strip the mask away and pass the final exam: What economist has tirelessly and eloquently reminded us that (positive) time preference is a necessary and sufficient condition for the emergence of the phenomenon we call interest and that the productivity of capital (or of waiting) is neither necessary nor sufficient for interest payments to occur? (*a*) Gustav Cassel, (*b*) Irving Fisher, (*c*) Frank Knight, (*d*) Murray Rothbard.

Professor Rothbard has taught us a theory of interest that allows us to sort out some of the thorniest issues in economic theory and in the history of economic thought. And he has used this theory as an important building block in his system of economics, which he in turn has integrated into a coherent view of social relationships. For all this we owe him our deepest gratitude.

Bibliography

Bailey, Samuel. *A Critical Dissertation on the Nature, Measure, and Causes of Value*. New York: Augustus M. Kelley, 1967 [1825].

Baird, Charles W. *Prices and Markets, Intermediate Microeconomics*. 2nd ed. St. Paul, Minn.: West Publishing, 1982.

Blaug, Mark. *The Cambridge Revolution: Success or Failure? A Critical Analysis of Cambridge Theories of Value and Distribution*. London: Institute of Economic Affairs, 1974.

Böhm-Bawerk, Eugen von. *Capital and Interest*. 4th ed. 3 vols. South Holland, Ill.: Libertarian Press, 1959 [1884–1912].

———. *Further Essays on Capital and Interest*. Spring Mills, Penn.: Libertarian Press, 1959 [1909–1912].

———. *History and Critique of Interest Theories*. Spring Mills, Penn.: Libertarian Press, 1959 [1884].

———. *Positive Theory of Interest*. Spring Mills, Penn.: Libertarian Press, 1959 [1889].

———. Review of Schumpeter's *Theorie der Wirtschaftlichen Entwicklung*. *Zeitschrift für Volkswirtschaft* (1913).

Bostaph, Samuel. "The Methodological Debate Between Carl Menger and the German Historicists." *Atlantic Economic Journal* 6, no. 3 (September, 1978).

Brown, H.G. "The Discount Versus the Cost-of-Production Theory of Capital Valuation." *American Economic Review* 4, no. 2 (June, 1914).

———. *Economic Science and the Common Welfare.* 3rd ed. Columbia, Mo.: Lucas Brothers, 1926.

———. "The Marginal Productivity versus the Impatience Theory of Interest." *Quarterly Journal of Economics* 27, no. 4 (August, 1913).

Cannan, Edwin. *A History of the Theories of Production and Distribution in English Political Economy from 1776 to 1848.* 3rd ed. London: P.S. King, 1924.

Cassel, Gustav. *The Nature and Necessity of Interest.* London: Macmillan, 1903.

Clark, John Bates. *The Distribution of Wealth.* New York: Macmillan, 1899.

Conard, J.W. *An Introduction to the Theory of Interest.* Berkeley and Los Angeles: University of California Press, 1959.

Dewey, Donald. *Modern Capital Theory.* New York and London: Columbia University Press, 1965.

Dorfman, Joseph. *The Economic Mind in American Civilization.* Vol. 3. New York: Viking Press, 1949.

Ely, Richard T., Thomas S. Adams, Max O. Lorenz, and Allyn A. Young. *Outlines of Economics.* 3rd ed. New York: Macmillan, 1920.

Fetter, Frank A. "Capital." In *Encyclopedia of the Social Sciences* 3. New York: Macmillan, 1930–1935. Reprinted in Fetter, *Capital, Interest, and Rent.*

———. *Capital, Interest, and Rent: Essays in the Theory of Distribution.* Murray N. Rothbard, ed. Kansas City: Sheed Andrews and McMeel, 1977.

———. "Capitalization versus Productivity: Rejoinder." *American Economic Review* 4, no. 4 (December, 1914).

———. *Economic Principles.* New York: The Century Co., 1915.

———. "Interest Theories, Old and New." *American Economic Review* 4, no. 1 (March, 1914). Reprinted in Fetter, *Capital, Interest, and Rent*. Murray N. Rothbard, ed. Kansas City: Sheed Andrews and McMeel, 1977.

———. "The Next Decade of Economic Theory." *Publications of the American Economic Association*. 3rd series, 2, no. 1 (February, 1901).

———. *Principles of Economics*. New York: The Century Co., 1904.

———. "Recent Discussion of the Capital Concept." *Quarterly Journal of Economics* 15, no. 1 (November, 1900).

———. "The Relations between Rent and Interest." *Publications of the American Economic Association*. 3rd series, 5, no. 1 (February, 1904).

———. Review of Eugen von Böhm-Bawerk's "Einige Strittige Fragen der Capitalstheorie." *Political Science Quarterly* 17, no. 1 (March, 1902).

———. Review of Irving Fisher's *"The Nature of Capital and Income." Journal of Political Economy* 15, no. 3 (March, 1907).

———. "The 'Roundabout Process' in the Interest Theory." *Quarterly Journal of Economics* 17, no. 1 (November, 1902). Reprinted in Fetter, *Capital, Interest, and Rent*. Murray N. Rothbard, ed. Kansas City: Sheed Andrews and McMeel, 1977.

Fisher, Irving. *Elementary Principles of Economics*. New York: Macmillan, 1911.

———. "Impatience Theory of Interest." *Scientia* 9 (1911).

———. [Reply] "The Impatience Theory of Interest." *American Economic Review* 3, no. 3 (September, 1913).

———. *The Nature of Capital and Income*. New York: Macmillan, 1906.

———. *The Rate of Interest: Its Nature, Determination, and Relation to Economic Phenomena*. New York: Macmillan Company, 1907.

———. *The Theory of Interest: As Determined by Impatience to Spend Income and Opportunity to Invest It*. New York: Macmillan Co., 1930.

Garrison, Roger W. "Comment: Waiting in Vienna." In *Time, Uncertainty, and Disequilibrium*. Mario J. Rizzo, ed. Lexington, Mass.: D.C. Heath, 1979.

———. "In Defense of the Misesian Theory of Interest." *Journal of Libertarian Studies* 3, no. 2 (Summer 1979).

———. "Professor Rothbard and the Theory of Interest." In *Man, Economy, and Liberty*. Walter Block and Llewellyn H. Rockwell, Jr., eds. Auburn, Ala.: Ludwig von Mises Institute, 1988.

Gordon, Barry. *Economic Analysis before Adam Smith: Hesiod to Lessius*. New York: Barnes & Noble, 1975.

Haavelmo, T. *A Study in the Theory of Investment*. Chicago: University of Chicago Press, 1960.

Hausman, Daniel M. *Capital, Profits and Prices*. New York: Columbia University Press, 1981.

Hayek, F.A. "The Mythology of Capital." *The Quarterly Journal of Economics* 50, no. 2 (February, 1936).

———. *Prices and Production and Other Works*. Auburn, Ala.: Ludwig von Mises Institute, 2008.

———. *The Pure Theory of Capital*. Chicago: University of Chicago Press, 1941.

———. "Time Preferences and Productivity: A Reconsideration." *Economica*, n.s., 12, no. 45 (February, 1945).

Hazlitt, Henry. *The Failure of the "New Economics."* Princeton, N.J.: D. Van Nostrand, 1959.

Hicks, John R. "Is Interest the Price of a Factor of Production?" In *Time, Uncertainty, and Disequilibrium*. Mario Rizzo, ed. Lexington, Mass.: D.C. Heath, 1979.

Hülsmann, Jörg Guido. "A Theory of Interest." *Quarterly Journal of Austrian Economics* 5, no. 4 (Winter 2002).

Hutchison, Terence W. *A Review of Economic Doctrines, 1870–1929*. Oxford: Clarendon Press, 1953.

Jevons, William Stanley. *The Theory of Political Economy.* 3rd ed. London: Macmillan, 1888 [1871].

Kauder, Emil. *A History of Marginal Utility Theory.* Princeton, N.J.: Princeton University Press, 1965.

Keynes, John Maynard. *The General Theory of Employment, Interest and Money.* New York: Harcourt, Brace and Company, 1936.

Kirzner, Israel M. *An Essay on Capital.* New York: Augustus M. Kelley Publishers, 1966.

———. "Pure Time Preference Theory: A Postscript to the 'Grand Debate.'" Manuscript, circa 1983.

———. "The PTPT of Interest: An Attempt at Clarification." In *The Meaning of Ludwig von Mises.* Jeffrey M. Herbener, ed. Auburn, Ala.: Ludwig von Mises Institute, 1993.

Knight, Frank H. "Capital, Time, and the Interest Rate." *Economica*, n.s. 1, no. 3 (August, 1934).

———. "Diminishing Returns from Investment." *Journal of Political Economy* 52, no. 1 (March, 1944).

Lachmann, Ludwig M. *Capital and Its Structure.* London: London School of Economics, 1956.

Longfield, S.M. *The Economic Writings of Mountifort Longfield.* R.D.C. Black, ed. Clifton, N.J.: Augustus M. Kelley, 1971.

Lutz, Friedrich A. *The Theory of Interest.* Chicago: Aldine Publishing, 1968.

Mankiw, N. Gregory. "It May Be Time for the Fed to Go Negative." *New York Times*, April 18, 2009.

Menger, Carl. *Principles of Economics.* James Dingwall and Bert Hoselitz, trans. New York: New York University Press, 1976 [1871].

Mises, Ludwig von. "A Critique of Böhm-Bawerk's Reasoning in Support of his Time Preference Theory." In Percy L. Greaves, Jr. *Mises Made Easier.* New York: Free Market Books, 1974.

———. *Human Action: A Treatise on Economics.* Scholar's edition. Auburn, Ala.: Ludwig von Mises Institute, 1998 [1949].

———. "The Rate of Interest." In *Human Action: A Treatise on Economics*. Scholar's Edition. Auburn, Ala.: Ludwig von Mises Institute, 1998.

Monroe, Arthur E. ed. *Early Economic Thought*. Cambridge, Mass.: Harvard University Press, 1924.

Moss, Laurence S. "The Emergence of Interest in a Pure Exchange Economy: Notes on a Theorem Attributed to Ludwig von Mises." In *New Directions in Austrian Economics*. Louis M. Spadaro, ed. Kansas City: Sheed Andrews and McMeel, 1978.

Murphy, Antoin E. *John Law: Economic Theorist and Policymaker*. Oxford: Oxford University Press, 1997.

Murphy, Robert P. *Unanticipated Intertemporal Exchange in Theories of Interest*. Doctoral Dissertation. New York: New York University, 2003.

Noonan, J.T., Jr. *The Scholastic Analysis of Usury*. Cambridge, Mass.: Harvard University Press, 1957.

O'Driscoll, Jr., Gerald P. "The Time Preference Theory of Interest Rate Determination." Paper presented at the meetings of the History of Economics Society. Toronto, 1978.

Pellengahr, Ingo. "Austrians Versus Austrians I: A Subjectivist View of Interest." In *Studies in Austrian Capital Theory, Investment and Time*. M. Faber, ed. Berlin, Heidelberg, and New York: Springer-Verlag, 1986.

———. "Austrians Versus Austrians II: Functionalist Versus Essentialist Theories of Interest." In *Studies in Austrian Capital Theory, Investment and Time*. M. Faber, ed. Berlin, Heidelberg, and New York: Springer-Verlag, 1986.

Radford, R.A. "The Economic Organization of a P.O.W. Camp." *Economica*, n.s., 12, no. 48 (November, 1945).

Rae, John. *Statement of Some New Principles on the Subject of Political Economy*. Boston: Hilliard, Gray, and Co., 1834.

Robbins, Lionel. "On a Certain Ambiguity in the Conception of Stationary Equilibrium." *The Economic Journal* 40, no. 158 (June, 1930).

Robinson, Joan. *Economic Philosophy*. Chicago: Aldine, 1962.

Rothbard, Murray. *Man, Economy, and State with Power and Market*. Scholar's Edition. Auburn, Ala.: Ludwig von Mises Institute, 2004 [1962].

———. "Time Preference." In *The New Palgrave Dictionary of Economics*. 2nd ed. Steven N. Durlauf and Lawrence E. Blume, eds. New York: Palgrave Macmillan, 2008.

Samuelson, Paul A. "Schumpeter as an Economic Theorist." In *Schumpeterian Economics*. H. Frisch, ed. New York: Praeger, 1981.

Schumpeter, Joseph. *Theorie der Wirtschaftlichen Entwicklung*. Munich: Duncker & Humblot, 1912.

———. *The Theory of Economic Development*. R. Opie, trans. Cambridge, Mass.: Harvard University Press, 1934.

Seager, H.R. [Comment] "The Impatience Theory of Interest," *American Economic Review* 3, no. 3 (September, 1913).

———. [Critique] "The Impatience Theory of Interest." *American Economic Review* 2, no. 4 (December, 1912).

Simkhovitch, V.G. "Hay and History." *Political Science Quarterly* 28, no. 3 (September, 1913).

Solow, Robert. "Cambridge and the Real World." *Times Literary Supplement* (March 14, 1975).

Stigler, George J. *The Theory of Price*. 3rd ed. New York: Macmillan, 1966.

Turgot, A.R.J. *The Economics of A.R.J. Turgot*. Peter D. Groenewegen, ed. The Hague: Martinus Nijhoff, 1977.

———. "Mémoire sur les prêts d'argent." Quoted in Peter D. Groenewegen, "A Reinterpretation of Turgot's Theory of Capital and Interest." *The Economic Journal* 81, no. 322 (June, 1971).

———. *Reflections on the Formation and Distribution of Wealth*. London: E. Spragg, 1793 [1774].

Whately, Richard. *Elements of Logic*. 9th ed. London: J.W. Parker, 1848.

Wicksell, Knut. "Böhm-Bawerk's Theory of Interest." In Knut Wicksell, *Selected Papers on Economic Theory*. E. Lindahl, ed. Cambridge, Mass.: Harvard University Press, 1958 [1911].

———. "The New Edition of Menger's *Grundsätze*." In Knut Wicksell, *Selected Papers on Economic Theory*. Erik Lindahl, ed. Cambridge, Mass.: Harvard University Press, 1958 [1924].

Yeager, Leland B. "Capital Paradoxes and the Concept of Waiting." In *Time, Uncertainty, and Disequilibrium*. Mario J. Rizzo, ed. Lexington, Mass.: D.C. Heath, 1979.

Index

A

agio theory of interest, 25, 38, 39, 134
American Economic Association, 133
Austrian School of Economics, 10, 64, 99, 165
Austrian theory of capital and interest, 61, 63, 86, 102, 160
autistic exchange, 92
Avvedimenti civili, 61

B

Bailey, Samuel, 63
Becker, Gary S., 87
Böhm-Bawerk, Eugen von, 12, 21–34, 35–40, 43, 45, 51, 56, 62, 64, 65, 66, 70, 72, 74, 100, 102, 104, 107, 108, 109, 110, 113, 114, 115, 116, 117, 118, 121, 126, 130, 133, 134, 144, 157, 166
  against the PTPT, 21–26
  criticism of Rae, 29–31
  theory of interest, 26–34
Brown, H.G., 108, 112, 127, 132, 140, 154, 155, 156, 157
Bush, George W., 7

C

Cambridge Capital Controversy, 122–25, 126
capital, 162
capital accumulation, 79, 80
Capital and Interest, 65
capital value, 140
capitalization, 12, 15, 16, 18, 20, 22, 34, 35, 39, 41, 42, 43, 44, 50, 51, 62, 138
  definition of, 62
capitalization theory of interest, 132–39, 151, 153, 154, 157

Cassel, Gustav, 165, 166, 172
causal-realist theory, 11, 12, 30, 36, 40, 46
central banking, 7, 9, 10
Clark, John B., 101, 156, 165
command of economic goods, 24, 25
Commentary on Usury, 60
contract interest, 12, 22, 147, 148, 151, 155
cost of money, 7
credit, 82
credit markets, 29
Crusoe, Robinson, 138

D

Della Moneta, 61
determining forces, 117
discounted marginal revenue product (DMRP), 46
discounting, 34, 44, 48, 161, 163, 164, 165, 168
Dorfman, Joseph, 43

E

Economic Principles, 49, 52
effective desire of accumulation, 27–29, 31
equilibrium rate of interest, 169, 170
evenly rotating economy, 75, 76, 77, 80, 83

F

Failure of the "New Economics," The, 9

Fetter, Frank, 12, 21–22, 35–57, 65, 66, 102, 105, 111
  defense of PTPT, 34–40
Fisher, Irving, 16, 35–40, 44, 51, 65, 87, 91, 93, 102, 103, 104, 107, 112, 115, 116, 117, 122, 127, 128, 129, 130, 131, 132, 140, 141, 142, 143, 144, 154, 156, 161, 169, 171, 172
Friedman, Milton, 161
"fructification theory of interest," 22, 62
future discount, 10, 14, 17
future goods, 59, 68
future utility, 32

G

Galiani, Ferdinando, 26, 61
Garrison, Roger, 44, 45, 52
Gesell, Silvio, 8

H

Hausman, Daniel M., 100
Hayek, Friedrich August von, 16, 36, 166, 171
Hazlitt, Henry, 9
History and Critique of Interest Theories, 21, 26
Hülsmann, Guido, 56, 57
human action, 13–15, 16, 30, 51, 66, 71, 89, 90, 92
  choice, 14, 16, 30, 34, 52
  means and ends, 13–14
Human Action: A Treatise on Economics, 51, 66

I

impatience theory of interest, 128
interest, 7, 10, 11, 12, 16, 18, 19, 21, 29, 30, 41, 43, 45, 49, 50, 54, 56, 62, 81
    as opportunity cost, 23, 37
    as payment for capital advances, 19, 20, 22–23
    as productivity return, 124
    definition, 67, 81, 137
    expressed as money, 42
    justification of, 60
    neoclassical view of, 124
    originary interest, 22, 67, 68, 69, 70–84
    uniform rate of interest, 15
interest income, 25, 111, 112, 113, 118, 120, 122, 125, 126
interest problem, 111, 112, 115, 127, 134, 156
interest rate, 7, 8, 10, 22, 29, 35, 44, 45, 48, 50, 51, 53, 55, 59, 67–84, 120, 140, 143, 151, 170
    as a price spread, 36
    as the price of waiting, 45, 165–68
    market-clearing, 45
    negative interest rates, 8
    positive interest rate, 85, 86
"Interest Theories New and Old," 35, 36
interest theory, 12, 26, 85, 115, 122, 135
internal financing, 90–95
intertemporal exchange, 90–95, 103, 109, 118, 121, 122, 124

J

Jevons, William Stanley, 12, 16, 26, 51

K

Keynes, John Maynard, 8, 9
Keynesians, 9, 10
Kirzner, Israel, 44, 45, 58, 166
Knies, Karl, 63
Knight, Frank, 44, 101, 107, 109, 112, 162, 163, 165, 166, 172
Kuznets, Simon, 111

L

Lachmann, Ludwig, 95
Law, John, 8, 9
liquidity, 9
loan pricing, 7
loans, 65, 131
    loan markets, 83
Longfield, Samuel Mountifort, 63
Lottini da Volterra, Gian Francesco, 61

M

Man, Economy, and State, 172
Mankiw, N. Gregory, 7, 8
marginal physical product (MPP), 46
marginal productivity, 65, 66, 169
    returns, 103
marginal revenue product (MRP), 46, 51
marginal utility, 52, 53, 135

marginal utility theory of price, 31
market economy, 15
market interest, 114, 115, 124, 126
market prices, 122, 143, 165, 165
Marx, Karl, 162, 163
Menger, Carl, 11, 12, 13, 16–18, 22, 23, 24, 26, 27, 35, 36, 64, 121
Menger's Law, 163
methodological essentialism, 120
Mill, James, 63
Mises, Ludwig von, 12, 16, 47, 51, 52, 53, 55, 56, 66, 85–98, 102, 105, 161, 166
  time preference theory, 89
Mississippi Bubble, 9
money, 48, 53, 55, 57
  and interest rates, 62
  as the common unit of value, 48, 49
  as an expression of wealth, 49
  tool of comparison, 47
Moss, Laurence S., 85–98
Murphy, Robert, 55

N

Navarrus, Martín de Azpilcueta, 60
negative interest rates, *see* interest rates
neoclassical theory, 85–98, 101, 123
New Directions in Austrian Economics, 85
numeraire money, 29

O

Occam's Razor, 169
originary interest, *see* interest definition, 70
originating forces, 117

P

Pellengahr, Ingo, 99
physical productivity, 109, 114, 116, 118, 119, 120, 121, 125, 126, 146, 170
Positive Theory of Capital, 65
positive time preference, *see* time preference
praxeological theory, 89, 90, 92, 94
preference, 15, 16
  for present goods over future goods, 28, 31–33, 38
present goods, 59, 63, 66, 68
price, 15, 16, 17, 46, 50, 51
  price theory, 11, 29, 122
Principles of Economics, 11, 26, 40, 49, 52, 64, 135
productivity of waiting theory, 102, 103, 107
productivity theory of interest, 65, 66, 69, 72, 73, 102, 114, 130, 131, 132, 144, 147, 152, 154
profit, 81, 123
  entrepreneurial profit, 81–83
psychic income, 40, 42, 43, 47, 136
psychological interest theories, 132, 141, 157
pure exchange economy, 85, 86, 98, 105, 119, 165
pure logic of choice, 87

pure rate of interest, 56, 57, 59
pure time preference, 32, 33, 35, 36, 39, 40, 45, 50, 52, 53, 55, 56, 57
Pure Time Preference Theory of Interest, 12, 16, 18, 21, 30, 37, 43–46, 51, 55–58, 99–126
  critics of, 55–58
  discounting, 17, 21, 22, 25
  Fetter's definition of, 40
  prehistory of, 16–21
  premium of the present vs. the future, 18, 27, 31
pure value productivity, 114, 116, 126

Q

Quesnay, François, 162, 163

R

Radford, R.A., 96
Rae, John, 26, 27, 28, 29, 30, 31, 35, 36, 37, 38, 64
Rate of Interest, The, 38, 132, 140, 142
rate of return, 60
rent, 11, 37, 40–41, 42, 43, 53, 67, 133, 134, 146
Robinson, Joan, 123
Rothbard, Murray, 18, 25, 51, 52, 55, 160, 161, 163, 165, 166, 167, 169, 170, 172

S

Samuelson, Paul, 44, 45, 107, 108, 111, 112

satisfaction preference, 16, 19, 32
  present vs. future, 16, 18, 31–32
saving, 75–80
Schumpeter, Joseph, 77, 100, 107, 108, 111, 112, 114, 162, 163
Seager, H.R., 127, 128, 130, 131, 140, 141, 142, 143, 144, 147, 148, 150, 151, 152, 154, 156, 157
Senior, Nassau, 165
Smith, Adam, 13
Solow, Robert, 123
Some New Principles on the Subject of Political Economy, 64
Statement of Some New Principles on the Subject of Political Economy, 26
Summenhart, Conrad, 60
surplus value, 162, 164

T

Theory of Interest, The, 38
Theory of Political Economy, The, 12, 13
time, 10, 14, 15, 25, 33, 95, 96, 97, 103, 107
  as waiting, 115, 126
time discount, 46, 49, 50, 51, 52, 53, 63, 68, 138, 145, 147, 153, 155
time preference, 10, 14, 15, 18, 21, 22, 25, 27, 28, 34, 35, 38, 49–53, 55, 59–66, 86, 87, 92, 103, 114, 116, 118, 119, 121, 140, 142, 143, 152, 155, 157, 161, 165, 170

and views of the future, 64
as affected by productivity, 28–29
collective time preference, 10
definition, 59
effect on interest rates, 62
"impatience," 142, 143, 154
neoclassical and Misesian, 87–98
neutral (zero) time preference, 87
positive, 103, 105, 107, 113, 120, 164
reason for, 27
time value, 46–47, 49, 50, 52, 53, 54, 55, 56, 137
Treatise on Contracts, 60
Turgot, A.R.J., 18–21, 22, 23, 26, 61, 62, 63

U

uniform rate of interest, 37
University of Heidelberg, 63
University of Salamanca, 60
University of Tübingen, 60
usury, 10, 60, 61

V

value, 44, 113
differentials, 92, 93
equivalent value, 47
independent cause of, 37
intertemporal differences in, 46
value productivity, 109, 114, 115, 116, 119, 120, 121, 126, 170
value theory, 96, 97, 111, 133

W

wages, 11, 123
Walras, Léon, 121, 162
wealth, 40–41, 43, 48, 49, 120, 136
Wicksell, Knut, 51

Y

Yeager, Leland, 165, 167